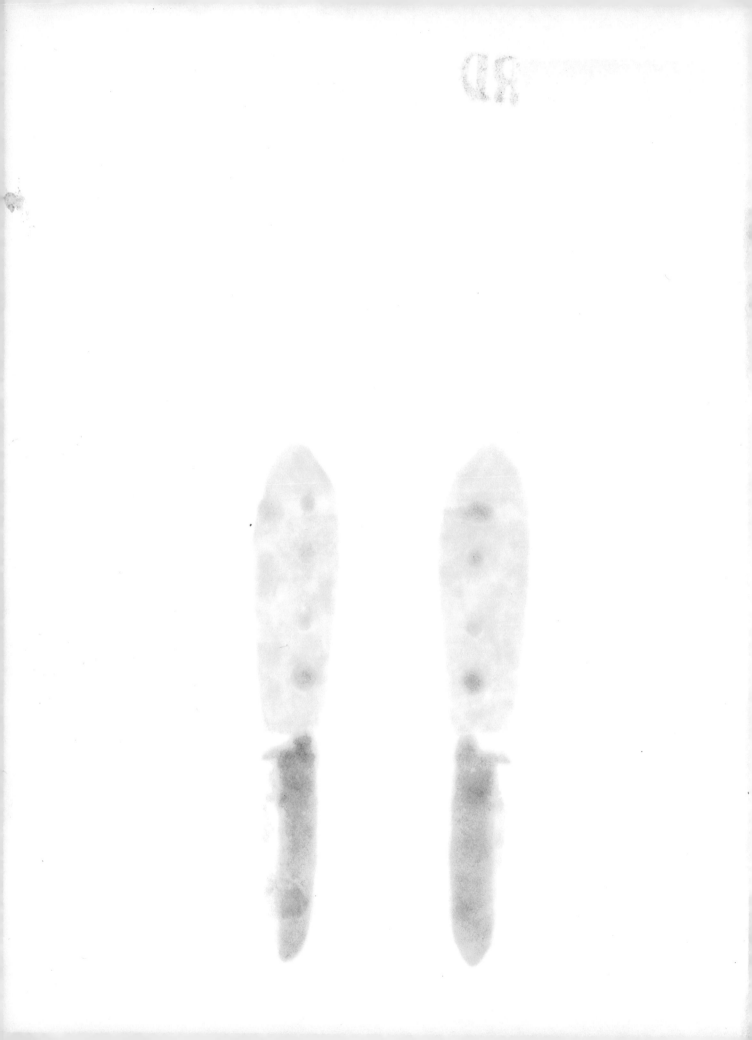

THE BIG BLUE SOUP BOOK

THE BIG BLUE SOUP BOOK

Ann Lerman

Illustration by Teresa Anderko

Running Press
Philadelphia, Pennsylvania

Canadian representatives: John Wiley & Sons Canada, Ltd.
22 Worcester Road, Rexdale, Ontario M9W 1L1

International representatives: Kaimon & Polon, Inc.
2175 Lemoine Avenue, Fort Lee, New Jersey 07024

9   8   7   6   5   4   3   2   1
Digit on right indicates the number of this printing.

Library of Congress Cataloging in Publication Data

Lerman, Ann, 1942–
  The big blue soup book.
  Includes indexes.
  SUMMARY: Includes recipes for twelve soup stocks and over 100 hot and cold soups.
  1. Soups—Juvenile literature. [1. Soups. 2. Cookery.] I. Title
  TX757.L43   641.8'13   78-1046
  ISBN 0-89471-033-8 Library binding
  ISBN 0-89471-032-x Paperback

Back cover text reproduced: By permission. From Webster's Third New International Dictionary © 1976 by G. & C. Merriam Co., Publishers of the Merriam-Webster Dictionaries.

Printed and bound by Port City Press, Baltimore, Maryland
Typography: Souvenir, by CompArt, Inc., Philadelphia, Pennsylvania

Cover and interior illustration by Teresa Anderko
Cover art direction by James Wizard Wilson
Editing by Alida Becker & Peter John Dorman

This book may be ordered directly from the publisher.
Please include 25 cents postage.

Try your bookstore first.

Running Press
38 South Nineteenth Street
Philadelphia, Pennsylvania 19103

First Words

Soup has an ancient and humble origin. Throughout history a loaf of bread and a bowl of soup have been nutritious staples. Whether homey or elegant, soup can include almost any ingredient and be enjoyed at any time of the day.

A flavorful soup starts with a stock rich in food value. When you're cooking, reserve all the liquids from vegetables; the liquids used for sprouting; fruit juices from drained, stewed, or soaked dried fruit; fish juices; and meat or poultry juices from which the fat has been removed. Refrigerate these nutritious liquids in covered jars and use them in any recipe in place of water. Adding raw vegetable scraps will also enhance the flavor and food value of your stock.

Before starting any of these recipes, assemble all the ingredients you'll need. This will aid in efficiency. It is also wise to use the items suggested in list of Basic Kitchen Equipment (p. xii) and in the recipes themselves.

You can prepare stocks well in advance, and they may be stored in the refrigerator or frozen. Don't remove the fat that rises to the surface until the stock is to be used; it seals out the air and helps to preserve the stock. Dehydrated chicken, beef, or vegetable broth (in cube or granular form) is a convenient alternative when homemade stock is not available. But be careful with the quantity of salt you use when preparing recipes with dehydrated broth; they tend to be overly salty. There are also several very good canned chicken and beef broths available. Try different brands to find one that suits you. Stocks that are not available commercially—those that can't be substituted for and must be made from the recipes in the first section of this book—will top the list of ingredients in the recipes that follow.

With a quantity of stock on hand, most of the soups in this book can be prepared quickly. Adding a variety of ingredients to a stock produces a soup that requires a minimum of cooking; in fact, these soups should be simmered only long enough for the ingredients to become tender. Fruits and vegetables that are cubed, diced, or shredded need only to be cooked in the stock for a very brief time. This method retains their nutritional value, color, and texture. Freshly made soups cooked this way should be served very soon after they've been prepared.

With the aid of a blender or food processor, you can whip up a delicious homemade soup in just minutes. Simply take fresh or frozen vegetables and combine them with a liquid—such as yogurt, broth, or juice—and blend until perfectly smooth. In minutes, the uncooked puréed vegetables are transformed into a fresh garden soup without losing any of their vitamins. These delicious instant-energy soups store well in a covered container in the refrigerator. Shake well before serving, and you have a quick, healthful drink.

Soups that are prepared with dried ingredients need a longer, slower cooking time. Soaking dried fruits or vegetables before using them will speed the process up a bit. Simmer these soups until the ingredients are very tender; this also gives the flavors time to blend.

Even if you've never made a soup before, it won't be long until you'll be tempted to add your own personal touch to a favorite recipe. An herb, vegetable, or starch will add flavor or create a new consistency. Yogurt, sour cream, buttermilk, and cream can all be interchanged or combined for variations of taste.

Don't let your imagination stop with the preparations. Serve soups at any time and present them in different ways to suit the season and occasion. Traditionally, soups mark the beginning of a meal. Served with a crusty loaf of bread, a hearty hot soup is a meal in itself. To give balance to a variety of dishes, a bouillon cup can be enjoyed throughout a meal. A light and refreshing chilled fruit soup is a delightful palate cleanser between courses. On a hot summer day, a chilled soup is a refreshing pick-me-up, while on a cold wintery day, hot soup served with a grilled sandwich can make a wholesome lunch. For a light conclusion to any meal, serve a fruit soup with a board of assorted cheeses.

Glass or white bowls will complement a chilled soup. Rest a glass bowl on a bed of crushed ice or serve your soup informally in a frosty mug. Hot soups are best in a warm tureen or warm earthenware bowls. A variety of garnishes will add nourishment as well as eye appeal. Snipped herbs, grated or chopped raw vegetables, nuts, seeds, blossoms, or thinly sliced fruits and vegetables will enhance the soup bowl or tureen.

However you serve them, or whichever ones you choose, enjoy a new ease in preparing, and delight in serving, soups in any season at any time.

—Annie Lerman

Contents

(Big Soups, cont'd)

Cream Sherry Consommé • Eggplant Soup Parmigiana • Cream Fruit Consommé • Onion Soup

VEGETARIAN SOUPS 55

Vegetable Barley Soup • Broccoli and Mushroom Soup • Brussels Sprout and Cheese Soup • Vegetable Soup with Eggs • Cheddar Cheese Soup • Chilled Orange Carrot Soup • Chilled Cucumber Soup • Iced Pea Soup • Creamy Pea Soup • Mushroom Barley Soup • Chilled Tomato Vegetable Soup • Dilled Potato and Onion Soup • Corn Chowder • Cold Beet and Cucumber Soup • Cool Cucumber and Red Onion Soup • Red Bean Soup with Rice • Chilled Artichoke Soup with Endive • Iced Green Bean Soup • Chilled Golden Squash Soup • Chilled Cauliflower Soup • Cream of Mushroom Soup • Chilled Green Summer Soup • Rice Soup • Sweet Potato Soup • Chilled Celery Soup • Creamed Spinach Soup • Celery Cabbage Soup • Chilled Avocado and Watercress Soup • Vegetable Chowder • Pumpkin Soup • Tomato Rice Soup • Chilled Blue Cheese Soup with Caviar • Alfalfa Sprout Soup with Mushrooms • Corn Soup • Strips of Cucumber Soup • Schav • Gazpacho • Split Pea Soup • Hearty Vegetable Soup

SEAFOOD SOUPS 85

Red Cod Chowder • Shrimp Gumbo • Vegetable Clam Chowder • Shrimp and Crab Soup • Herbed Spinach Soup • Chilled Shrimp Bisque • Crab Gumbo • Chilled Lobster Bisque • Clam Bisque • White Clam Chowder • Red Clam Chowder • Chilled Clam and Avocado Soup • Bouillabaisse • Chilled Salmon Bisque • Oyster Soup • Clam and Mushroom Soup •

Glossary of Cooking Terms

Bisque: a thick cream soup, often made from fish or vegetable purées.

Blend: to mix smoothly and inseparably together.

Boil: to heat or cook in a liquid whose temperature reaches 212 degrees F; the surface will be broken by a steady bubbling action.

Bouillabaisse: a soup or stew containing several kinds of fish and shellfish; usually prepared with oil, tomatoes and spices.

Bouillon: a clear seasoned broth made from poultry, meat, fish, or vegetables; also commercially prepared bouillon dissolved in boiling water.

Bouillon cube: a small cube of dehydrated beef, chicken, or vegetable stock.

Bouillon cup: a small vessel with two handles in which bouillon is served.

Bouquet garni: a small bundle of herbs wrapped and tied together in a piece of cheesecloth.

Broth: water that has been boiled with meat, fish, or vegetables and then strained.

Chill: to make cold, not frozen, in the refrigerator.

Chop: to cut into small pieces.

Chowder: a soup or stew made of fish or vegetables which contains potatoes and onions, among other ingredients and seasonings.

Clarify: to make a substance pure or clear.

Coconut milk: a liquid obtained from fresh coconut meat.

Coconut water: the liquid within the fruit of the fresh coconut.

Consommé: a strong clear soup made by simmering meat and bones to extract their nutritive properties.

Combine: to mix or blend together two or more ingredients.

Cool: to allow to stand until heat has reduced.

Crouton: a small piece of fried or toasted bread used in soups as a garnish.

Crush: to mash fruits and vegetables, for example, until they lose their shape.

Cube: to cut into small, equal squares.

Dice: to cut into very small, even cubes 1/4 to 1/2 inch long.

Drain: to remove liquid, usually by allowing food to stand in a strainer or colander until liquid has drained off.

Flake: to break into small pieces with a fork, as with cooked fish.

Froth: an aggregation of bubbles formed in or on an agitated liquid.

Garnish: to decorate or accompany a dish by adding other foodstuffs, such as snipped herbs.

Grate: to reduce a food to small particles by rubbing it on the teeth of a grater.

Gumbo: a stew or thick soup containing okra.

Julienne: food, such as carrots or cheese, cut into thin, matchlike strips.

Madrilene: a consommé flavored with tomato, frequently jelled and served cold.

Mince: to cut or chop into very fine pieces.

Mix: to blend or stir together two or more ingredients.

Peel: 1. to remove the skin or rind of a fruit or vegetable with a knife or other peeling tool 2. the skin or rind of a fruit or vegetable.

Pith: the white membrane under the rind of citrus fruits.

Poach: to cook food in a liquid that is barely simmering.

Potage: the French word for soup.

Preheat: to heat an oven or broiler to a desired temperature before using; usually takes about 10 minutes.

Purée: to force food through a sieve or food mill (or process in a blender or food processor) to obtain a thick, smooth liquid.

Refresh: to plunge hot food into cold water, quickly stopping the cooking process.

Rind: the outer skin of a fruit or vegetable.

Sauté: to cook briefly in a small amount of hot fat.

Scramble: to cook in a pan, mixing quickly.

Shred: to cut or break into thin pieces.

Sieve: 1. to put or force through a sieve 2. a sieved or processed food.

Simmer: to cook a liquid barely at the boiling point; the surface should show only a few bubbles breaking slowly.

Skim: to remove a substance from the surface of a liquid.

Stock: a strained liquid in which meat, poultry, fish, bones, or vegetables and seasonings have been (or will be) cooked.

Tender: soft or delicate in substance; cooked to a delicate or soft texture.

Whisk: to whip with a whisk or other beating implement.

Basic Kitchen Equipment

Chopping *or* **cutting board:** 1. made of durable hardwood about one inch thick. 2. acrylic, thought by many to be more sanitary.

Electric blender: for grinding, grating, puréeing, and blending food.

Electric food processor: accomplishes all the jobs of an electric blender and many others.

Food mill: for puréeing, mashing, and grinding almost any food; can be used instead of blender or food processor.

Grater: for grating and slicing; the best model stands upright and has several sizes of teeth and a slicer.

Kettle: a large heavy pot with a cover, about 8-10 quart capacity.

Knives: 1. chopping—a wide 8 inch blade for chopping, mincing, and dicing fruits, vegetables, and meat. 2. paring—a 3 to 3 1/2 inch blade for peeling and cutting small fruits and vegetables. 3. utility—a 5 to 7 inch blade for peeling and chopping large fruits and vegetables, and trimming meat.

Measuring cups: 1. glass for measuring liquids; 1 cup size and 1 quart size, with pouring lip. 2. metal for measuring solids; a graduated set of 1/4 cup, 1/3 cup, 1/2 cup, and 1 cup.

Measuring spoons: a standard set of 1/4 teaspoon, 1/2 teaspoon, 1 teaspoon, and 1 tablespoon; a second set comes in handy.

Mixing bowls: glass, pottery, or stainless steel; a graduated set of sizes.

Saucepans: 2 quart, 3 to 3 1/2 quart, and 5 quart; all with covers.

Sieve: an instrument with a meshed or perforated bottom, used for straining liquids.

Tureen: a deep covered vessel from which cooked foods are served at the table.

Whisk: wire or wooden; an implement, usually loops held together in a handle, for beating and whipping; 8-10 inch size.

Wooden spoons: unvarnished wood for beating and stirring; 10-12 inch size.

STOCKS

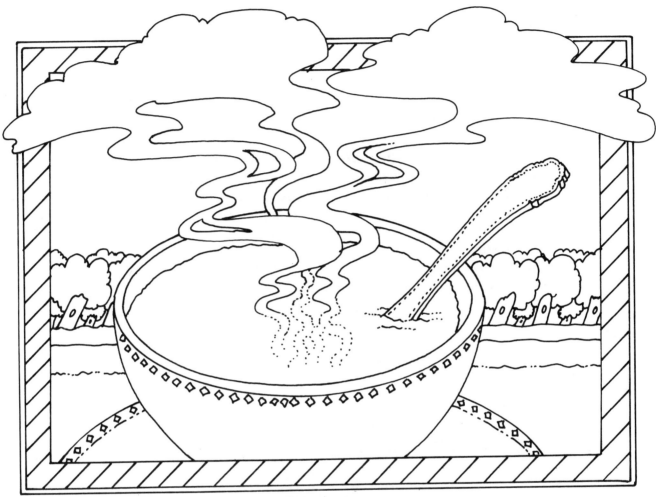

Giblet Stock

giblets from 1 fowl, omit liver
1 cup water
1 cup chicken stock
1 small onion

1 small carrot
bouquet garni of 3 sprigs parsley,
   1 sprig thyme, 1/2 bay leaf
salt to taste

Combine giblets, water, and chicken stock in saucepan. Bring to boil. Skim off froth as it rises to surface. Lower heat to simmer. Add onion, carrot, and bouquet garni. Cover and simmer mixture for about 1 hour. Add salt to taste.

Remove and discard bouquet garni. Strain stock through fine sieve, pressing hard on solids. Cool stock at room temperature. Chill in covered container for later use. Stock may be frozen.

Makes about one and a half cups.

Turkey Stock

1 roasted turkey carcass,
  broken
3 quarts water
1 onion
1 carrot
1 leek

1 turnip, chopped
1 tablespoon salt
bouquet garni of 6 sprigs
    parsley, 2 sprigs thyme, 1
    bay leaf, and 4 peppercorns
salt to taste

Combine turkey carcass and water in large kettle. Bring to boil. Skim off froth as it rises to surface. Lower heat to simmer. Add onion, carrot, leek, turnip, salt, and bouquet garni. If necessary add boiling water to keep ingredients barely covered. Cover and simmer mixture for about 2 1/2 hours. Add salt to taste.

Remove and discard carcass and bouquet garni. Strain stock through fine sieve, pressing hard on solids.

Cool stock at room temperature. Chill in covered container for later use. Stock may be frozen.

Makes about two and a half quarts.

Annie's Tips

Place ingredients for bouquet garni in the center of a square piece of cheesecloth. Fold cheesecloth in half. Sew edges together with white thread. Leave a six-inch-long thread to hang over edge of pot.

Bouquet garni may be prepared in a tea ball if fresh herbs and seeds are used.

Chicken Stock

3 quarts water
4 pounds chicken, disjointed,
    and giblets, omit liver
1 large onion
2 carrots
2 stalks celery, halved

1 tablespoon salt
bouquet garni of 6 sprigs
    parsley, 2 sprigs thyme, 1
    bay leaf, and 4 peppercorns
salt to taste

Bring water to boil in large kettle. Add chicken and giblets. Skim off froth as it rises to surface. Lower heat to simmer. Add onion, carrots, celery, salt, and bouquet garni. If necessary add boiling water to keep ingredients barely covered. Cover and simmer mixture for about 1 1/2 hours.

Remove chicken from kettle. Remove meat from carcass, reserving for later use. Return carcass to kettle and continue to simmer for about 1 hour. Add salt to taste.

Remove and discard carcass and bouquet garni. Strain stock through fine sieve, pressing hard on solids.

Cool stock at room temperature. Chill in covered container for later use. Do not remove fat that rises to surface until stock is to be used. Stock may be frozen.

Makes about two and a half quarts.

Coconut Milk

(not coconut water)

3 cups water
2 cups unsweetened coconut,
    grated

Put water in saucepan. Stir in coconut. Bring mixture to boil.

Remove saucepan from heat. Cover and allow to stand for 30 minutes.

Strain coconut mixture through sieve lined with double thickness of cheesecloth. Squeeze cheesecloth to extract all coconut milk.

Cool coconut milk at room temperature. Chill coconut milk in covered container for later use. Coconut milk may be used at once. (Before using prepared chilled coconut milk, heat to blend.)

Makes about two and a half cups.

Basic Fish Stock

1–1 1/2 pounds whole fish, cut into large pieces (such as flounder, haddock, sole, whiting, or tile)
2 stalks celery and tops, sliced
1 onion, sliced
1 carrot, sliced
1/2 teaspoon salt
bouquet garni of 1 bay leaf, 1/4 teaspoon fennel seeds, 1/4 teaspoon dill seeds, 2 table-spoons dried parsley leaves, and 1/4 teaspoon dulse (optional)
4 cups water
salt and pepper to taste

Combine fish, celery, onion, carrot, salt, and bouquet garni in heavy saucepan. Add water. If necessary add more water to cover ingredients. Bring to boil. Lower heat. Cover and simmer for about 30 minutes.

Remove and discard bouquet garni. Add salt and pepper to taste.

Strain stock through fine sieve, pressing hard on solids.

Cool stock at room temperature. Chill in covered container for later use. Stock may be frozen. Basic fish stock may be used at once.

Makes about three and a half cups.

Bouillon

3 1/2 quarts water
2 pounds chicken, disjointed
2 pounds lean brisket
2 pounds shin bones
2 teaspoons salt
1/8 teaspoon cayenne

bouquet garni of 1 bay leaf, 6
   sprigs parsley, 2 peppercorns, and 2 sprigs thyme
1 onion
2 carrots, trimmed
1 stalk celery and top, halved
salt to taste

Combine water, chicken, brisket, and bones in large kettle. Bring to boil. Skim off froth as it rises to surface. Lower heat to simmer. Add salt, cayenne, bouquet garni, onion, carrots, and celery. If necessary add boiling water to keep ingredients barely covered. Cover and simmer for about 1 1/2 hours.

Remove brisket and chicken parts from kettle. Remove meat from chicken bones. Reserve brisket and chicken for later use.

Return chicken bones to kettle. Cover and simmer for about 1 hour. Add salt to taste.

Remove and discard shin bones, chicken bones, and bouquet garni. Strain bouillon through fine sieve, pressing hard on solids.

Cool bouillon at room temperature. Chill in covered container for later use. Do not remove fat that rises to surface until bouillon is to be used. Bouillon may be frozen.

Makes about three quarts.

Annie's Tips

Draw a spoon across the surface of the hot liquid to skim froth.

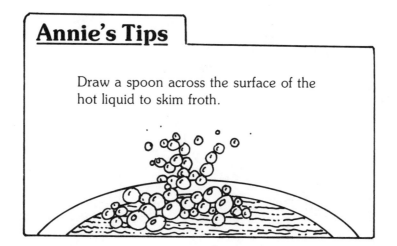

Green Vegetable Stock

6 cups water
1/4 cup dried mushrooms, rinsed
1/2 cup split peas, green or yellow
1/2 pound fresh mushrooms, soaked and wiped
1 large potato, cut into chunks
1 onion
2 carrots, cut into chunks

2 stalks celery, with tops, cut into chunks
1 cup green beans, snapped
2 zucchini, cut into chunks
4 sprigs parsley
1 1/2 teaspoons salt
1/4 cup nutritional yeast (optional)
salt and pepper to taste

Combine water, dried mushrooms, and split peas in large saucepan. Bring to boil. Lower heat. Cover and simmer for about 1 hour.

Add mushrooms, potato, onion, carrots, celery, green beans, zucchini, and parsley. Bring to boil. Lower heat. Cover and simmer for about 30 minutes.

Strain stock through sieve lined with double thickness of cheesecloth. Squeeze cheesecloth to extract all of stock. Return stock to saucepan. Stir in salt and nutritional yeast. Add salt and pepper to taste.

Cool stock at room temperature. Chill in covered container for later use. Green Vegetable Stock may be used at once. Stock may be frozen.

Makes about five cups.

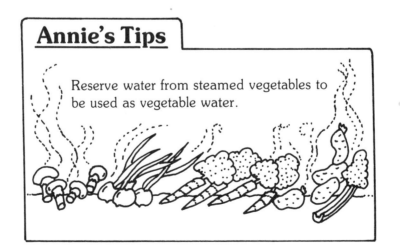

Annie's Tips

Reserve water from steamed vegetables to be used as vegetable water.

Beef Stock

3 pounds beef with bones
3 quarts water
1 onion
1 carrot
1 stalk celery, halved
1 tomato, quartered

1 tablespoon salt
bouquet garni of 6 sprigs
   parsley, 4 peppercorns, and 2
   sprigs thyme
salt to taste

Combine beef with bones and water in kettle. Bring to boil. Skim off froth as it rises to surface. Lower heat to simmer. Add onion, carrot, celery, tomato, salt, and bouquet garni. If necessary add boiling water to keep ingredients barely covered. Cover and simmer mixture for about 1 1/2 hours. Add salt to taste.

Remove beef with bones and reserve beef for later use. Remove and discard bouquet garni. Strain stock through fine sieve, pressing hard on solids.

Cool stock at room temperature. Chill in covered container for later use. Do not remove fat that rises to surface until stock is to be used. Stock may be frozen.

Makes about two and a half quarts.

Vegetable Stock

6 cups water
4 carrots, sliced
1 onion
2 stalks celery, halved
2 leeks, cut into chunks
1/2 pound green beans, snapped

2 zucchini, sliced
2 tomatoes, cut into chunks
1/2 pound mushroom stems
4 sprigs parsley
1 1/2 tablespoons soy sauce

Combine all ingredients except soy sauce in kettle. Bring to boil. Lower heat to simmer. Cover and simmer for about 1 hour. Add soy sauce. Cover and simmer for about 10 minutes.

Strain stock through sieve lined with double thickness of cheesecloth. Squeeze cheesecloth to extract all stock.

Cool stock at room temperature. Chill in covered container for later use. Stock may be frozen. Vegetable stock may be used at once.

Makes about seven cups.

Lamb Stock

2 pounds lamb shanks, cracked
7 cups water
1 onion
1 carrot
1 stalk celery, halved

1 teaspoon salt
bouquet garni of 1 bay leaf, 3
    sprigs parsley, and 2 pepper-
    corns
salt to taste

Combine lamb shanks and water in kettle. Bring to boil. Skim off froth as it rises to surface. Lower heat to simmer. Add onion, carrot, celery, salt, and bouquet garni. If necessary add boiling water to keep ingredients barely covered. Cover and simmer mixture for about 2 hours. Add salt to taste.

Remove lamb shanks, reserving lamb for later use. Remove and discard bouquet garni. Strain stock through fine sieve, pressing hard on solids.

Cool stock at room temperature. Chill in covered container for later use. Do not remove fat that rises to surface until stock is to be used. Stock may be frozen.

Makes about one and a half quarts.

White Fish Stock

2 tablespoons salad oil
1 onion, sliced
1 pound fish, bones, and skin
    from any white fish (such as
    flounder, sole, or whiting)
4 cups water
1 carrot

1/2 teaspoon salt
bouquet garni of 12 sprigs
    parsley and 1/2 bay leaf
3 tablespoons lemon juice
1/2 cup dry white wine
salt and pepper to taste

Combine salad oil and onion in heavy saucepan. Sauté for about 2 minutes or until onions are crisp tender. Stir in fish, bones, fish skin, and water. Bring mixture to boil. Skim off froth as it rises to surface. Lower heat to simmer. Add carrot, salt, bouquet garni, lemon juice, and wine. If necessary add boiling water to keep ingredients barely covered. Cover and simmer for about 25 minutes. Add salt and pepper to taste.

Remove and discard bouquet garni. Strain stock through fine sieve, pressing hard on solids.

Cool stock at room temperature. Chill in covered container for later use. White fish stock may be used at once.

Makes about four cups.

Puréed Fish Stock

2 large onions, sliced
4 tablespoons salad oil
3 pounds assorted fish steaks
   (bass, whiting, porgy, sole,
   tile)
4 large tomatoes, cut into
   chunks

1 quart water
1 teaspoon salt
bouquet garni of 6 sprigs
   thyme, 6 sprigs parsley, 1
   bay leaf, and 4 peppercorns
salt to taste

Combine onions and salad oil in kettle. Sauté for about 2 minutes or until onions are crisp tender. Stir in fish steaks and tomatoes. Continue stirring and simmer for about 10 minutes. Stir in water, salt, and bouquet garni. Bring mixture to boil. Lower heat and simmer in covered kettle for about 20 minutes.

Remove and discard bouquet garni and any heavy bones that may be in stock.

In batches, transfer fish mixture to blender or food processor. Blend until smooth.

Return purée to kettle. Simmer for 5 minutes. Add salt to taste.

Cool puréed stock at room temperature. Chill in covered container for later use. Stock may be frozen. Puréed fish stock may be used at once.

Makes about three quarts.

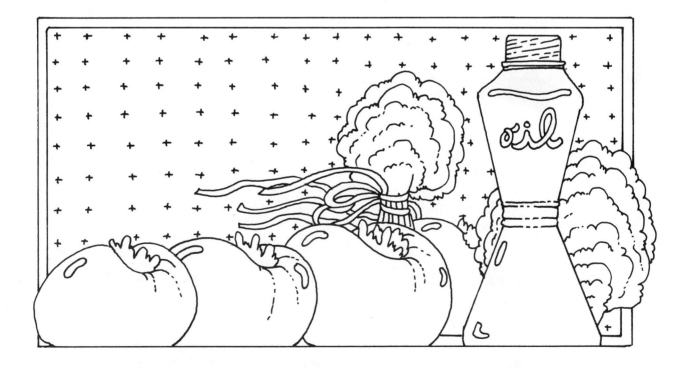

Consommé

3 quarts water
3 pounds chicken, disjointed
1 pound lean beef
1 pound veal bones
1 pound marrow bones
2 teaspoons salt
1/4 teaspoon celery salt
1/4 teaspoon nutmeg

bouquet garni of 4 peppercorns,
   2 sprigs thyme, and 6 sprigs
   parsley
1 onion
2 carrots, trimmed
2 stalks celery and tops, halved
salt to taste

Combine water and chicken in large kettle. Bring to boil. Skim off froth as it rises to surface. Lower heat to simmer. Add beef, veal bones, marrow bones, salt, celery salt, nutmeg, bouquet garni, onion, carrots, and celery. If necessary add boiling water to keep ingredients barely covered. Cover and simmer for about 4 hours. Add salt to taste.

Remove chicken and beef. Remove and discard bones and bouquet garni. Strain consommé through sieve lined with double thickness of cheesecloth. Press hard on solids.

Cool consommé at room temperature. Chill in covered container for later use. Do not remove fat that rises to surface until consommé is to be used. Consommé may be frozen.

Makes about two and a half quarts.

BIG SOUPS

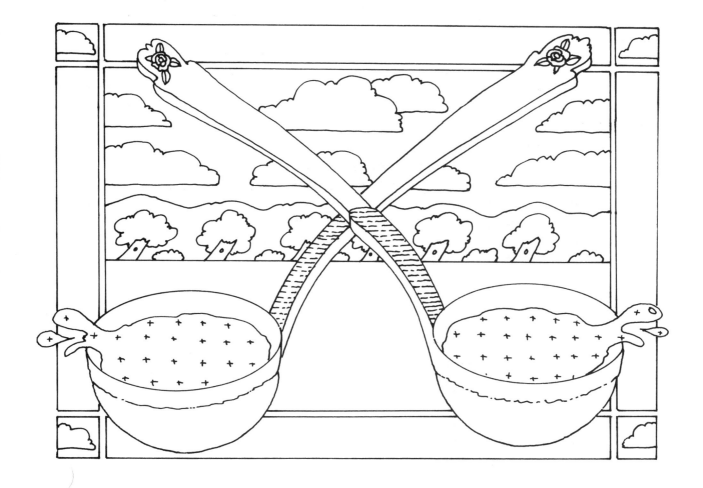

Split Pea Soup

2 cups beef stock
6 cups water
2 cups dried split peas

bouquet garni of 1 bay leaf and
   1 teaspoon thyme
3 carrots, chopped fine
2 tablespoons dried parsley

   In large saucepan combine beef stock, water, dried split peas, and bouquet garni. Bring mixture to boil. Lower heat, cover, and simmer for 1 1/2 hours. Add carrots. Simmer uncovered for 20 minutes. Stir occasionally.
   Remove and discard bouquet garni. Stir in parsley.
   Serve soup in warm tureen or warm individual soup bowls.
   Makes six servings.

Jelled Cranberry Bouillon Cup

1/4 cup cold water
1 tablespoon unflavored gelatin
2 cups turkey stock
1 cup jellied cranberry sauce

2 whole cloves
salt and pepper to taste
5 slices lemon
bread sticks

Combine water and gelatin in small bowl. Set aside for 5 minutes.

Combine turkey stock, cranberry sauce, gelatin mixture, and cloves in saucepan. Bring to boil. Lower heat and simmer for about 5 minutes, or until smooth. Add salt and pepper to taste.

Strain mixture through fine sieve. Divide bouillon between 5 bouillon cups. Chill for about 4 hours.

Break up jelled bouillon with fork before serving. Garnish with lemon slice on edge of each cup. Serve with bread sticks.

Makes five servings.

Cream of Tomato Soup

3 tablespoons margarine
1 onion, chopped
3 cups tomatoes, canned or
   fresh, chopped
1/2 teaspoon salt
1 teaspoon sugar
2 tablespoons flour

1/4 teaspoon baking soda
1 cup chicken stock
1 cup sour cream
salt and pepper to taste
snipped dill or fresh minced
   basil

Combine margarine and onion in saucepan. Sauté onion for about 3 minutes, or until tender.

Transfer onion to blender or food processor. Add tomatoes, salt, sugar, flour, and baking soda. Blend until smooth.

Transfer tomato mixture to saucepan. Stir in chicken stock and sour cream. Stir and heat soup to simmer. Do not boil. Add salt and pepper to taste.

Serve soup in warm tureen or warm individual soup bowls. Garnish with snipped dill or minced basil.

Makes four servings.

Chilled Cucumber Soup

1 cup chicken stock
1/2 cup currants or raisins
1/3 cup ground walnuts
1 cup yogurt
1 cup light cream or half-and-half
1 hard-boiled egg, minced

1/4 cup scallions, white part only, chopped fine
1 cucumber, peeled and chopped
salt and pepper to taste
snipped dill

Combine chicken stock and currants in saucepan. Bring to boil. Remove from heat. Set aside.

Combine walnuts, yogurt, light cream, egg, scallions, and cucumber in mixing bowl. Whisk in currant mixture.

Chill in covered container for about 4 hours. Add salt and pepper to taste.

Serve in glass bowls. Garnish with snipped dill.

Makes four servings.

Annie's Tips

Cold soup requires more seasoning than hot soup. Taste test the soup after chilling.

Barley and Vegetable Soup

4 cups chicken stock
1/3 cup barley
3 tablespoons margarine
2 stalks celery, chopped
2 carrots, chopped
1 leek, chopped

1 tablespoon margarine
1/2 pound mushrooms, soaked,
   wiped, and chopped
salt and pepper to taste
1/2 cup chopped parsley

Heat chicken stock in saucepan. Bring stock to boil. Add barley. Lower heat. Cover and simmer for about 20 minutes.

In skillet sauté celery, carrots, and leek in 3 tablespoons margarine for 2 minutes. Add mixture to saucepan. Sauté mushrooms in 1 tablespoon margarine for 1 minute. Add mushrooms to saucepan.

Simmer soup for 15 minutes, or until barley and vegetables are tender. Add salt and pepper to taste.

Serve soup in warm tureen or warm individual soup bowls. Garnish with chopped parsley.

Makes four servings.

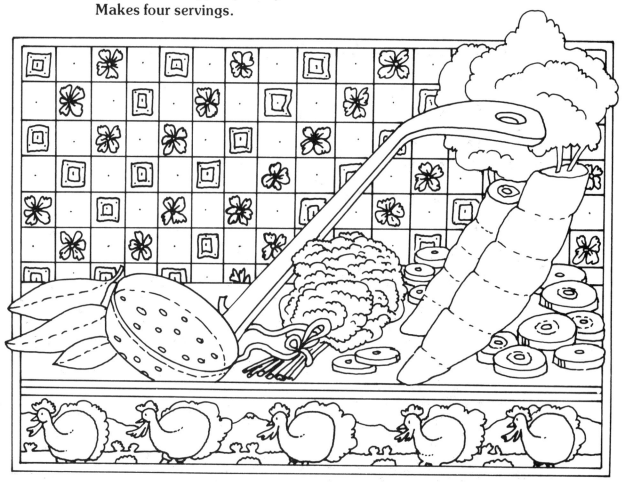

Buckwheat and Potato Soup

4 cups chicken stock
2 large potatoes, peeled and
    diced
1 large onion, chopped
1/4 cup medium buckwheat
    groats

salt and pepper to taste
1 cup evaporated milk
1 teaspoon dried parsley flakes
1 teaspoon dried thyme

Combine chicken stock, potatoes, onion, and buckwheat groats in covered saucepan. Bring mixture to boil. Lower heat and simmer for about 12 minutes, or until potatoes are tender. Add salt and pepper to taste. Stir in evaporated milk, parsley, and thyme. Simmer soup for 5 minutes. Do not boil.

Serve soup in warm tureen or warm individual soup bowls.

Makes four servings.

Asparagus Potato Chowder

2 cups chicken stock
3 medium red-skinned potatoes,
    peeled and diced
1 small onion, chopped
1/2 teaspoon salt
1/8 teaspoon ground nutmeg

10 ounce package frozen cut
    asparagus
salt and pepper to taste
1 1/2 cups half-and-half or light
    cream
4 ounce package cream cheese
    with pimiento, softened

Combine chicken stock, potatoes, onion, salt, and nutmeg in saucepan. Bring mixture to boil. Lower heat. Cover and simmer for about 5 minutes Add frozen asparagus and return mixture to boil. Lower heat. Cover and simmer for about 5 minutes, or until vegetables are crisp tender. Add salt and pepper to taste.

In mixing bowl blend softened cream cheese with half-and-half or light cream. Stir mixture into saucepan. Continue stirring until blended. Do not boil.

Serve at once in warm tureen or warm individual soup bowls.

Makes four servings.

Chilled Garden Madrilène

2 1/2 cups crushed tomatoes
2 1/2 cups consommé
2 tablespoons dry sherry
1 stalk celery, minced
1 small onion, minced
1 small carrot, minced
1/2 medium cucumber, minced

1/2 medium green pepper,
  minced
1/2 teaspoon salt
1 sprig parsley, minced
1/4 teaspoon thyme, crushed
salt and pepper to taste
sour cream

Combine all ingredients except sour cream in mixing bowl. Chill in covered container for about 4 hours. Add salt and pepper to taste.

Serve in glass bowls. Garnish with dollops of sour cream.

Makes six servings.

Annie's Tips

If a jelled madrilène is desired, combine 1 tablespoon unflavored gelatin and ½ cup water. Add softened gelatin to soup before chilling.

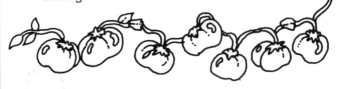

Japanese Mushroom Soup

4 cups chicken stock
1/4 pound mushrooms, soaked,
   wiped, and sliced very thin
1 medium onion, sliced very
   thin
1 cinnamon stick

1/8 teaspoon ground nutmeg
salt and pepper to taste
1 tablespoon cornstarch
1/4 cup cold water
1/4 cup chopped parsley

In saucepan combine stock, mushrooms, onion, cinnamon stick, and nutmeg. Bring to boil. Reduce heat and simmer for 15 minutes. Remove cinnamon stick. Add salt and pepper to taste.

Combine cornstarch and cold water. Stir cornstarch mixture into hot soup. Continue stirring until soup has thickened slightly and is clear.

Serve soup in warm tureen or warm individual soup bowls. Garnish with chopped parsley.

Makes four servings.

Annie's Tips

Soak mushrooms in cold water for 5 minutes before wiping.

Chicken Fried Rice Soup

4 cups chicken stock
1/4 cup salad oil
1/4 cup scallions, sliced thin
1 stalk celery, chopped
2 cloves garlic, minced

1 large egg, beaten
1 cup cooked rice
1/4 cup bean sprouts
2 tablespoons soy sauce
crisp Oriental noodles

Heat chicken stock in saucepan to simmer.

Combine salad oil, scallions, celery, and garlic in skillet. Sauté mixture for about 3 minutes. Add egg and scramble. Add rice, bean sprouts, and soy sauce to egg mixture. Add rice mixture to chicken stock.

Serve soup in warm tureen or warm individual soup bowls. Garnish with crisp Oriental noodles.

Makes four servings.

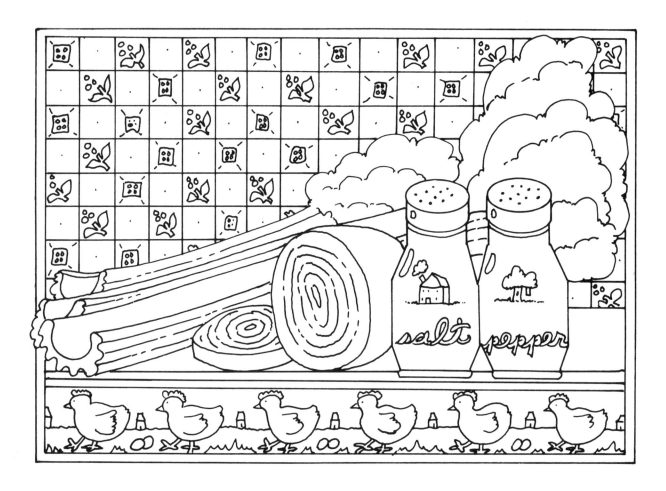

Turkey and Barley Soup

3 tablespoons salad oil
1 onion, minced
2 tablespoons salad oil
1 small carrot, diced
1 stalk celery, diced
1 cup mushrooms, soaked,
    wiped, and chopped

6 1/2 cups turkey stock
1/4 cup pearl barley
3/4 teaspoon marjoram
1/4 teaspoon salt
salt and pepper to taste

Combine 3 tablespoons salad oil and onion in large saucepan. Sauté onion for about 2 minutes. Add 2 tablespoons salad oil, carrot, celery, and mushrooms. Sauté for about 5 minutes. Add turkey stock, barley, marjoram, and salt. Bring mixture to boil. Lower heat. Cover and simmer, stirring occasionally, for about 1 hour and 15 minutes, or until barley is very tender. Add salt and pepper to taste.

Serve soup in warm tureen or warm individual soup bowls.

Makes six servings.

Apricot Lentil Soup

6 cups lamb stock or beef stock
1 onion, diced
1 cup lentils, rinsed
1/2 teaspoon salt
2 medium potatoes, peeled and
    diced

1 cup dried apricots, diced
1/3 cup chopped walnuts
1/2 teaspoon tarragon
salt and pepper to taste

Combine lamb stock, onion, lentils, and salt in large saucepan. Bring to boil. Lower heat. Cover and simmer for about 1 hour. Add potatoes, apricots, walnuts, and tarragon. Cover and simmer for about 20 minutes, or until potatoes are tender. Add salt and pepper to taste.

Serve soup in warm tureen or warm individual soup bowls.

Makes six servings.

Sweet-Sour Cabbage Borscht

2 tablespoons salad oil
1 onion, diced
8 cups beef stock
1 pound can tomatoes, crushed
1/4 cup raisins
1 large head cabbage, shredded

1/2 teaspoon salt
1/4 teaspoon ground ginger
1/4 cup lemon juice
1/4 cup honey
honey or lemon juice to taste
salt and pepper to taste

Combine salad oil and onion in large saucepan. Sauté onion for about 2 minutes. Add beef stock, tomatoes, raisins, cabbage, and salt. Bring to boil. Lower heat. Cover and simmer for about 10 minutes. Stir in ginger, lemon juice, and honey. Continue to simmer for about 10 minutes. Add either honey or lemon juice to taste. Add salt and pepper to taste.

Serve soup in warm tureen or warm individual soup bowls.

Makes eight servings.

Annie's Tips

Chopped or shredded vegetables that will be added to soup only need to be cooked briefly. This method retains their food value.

Tomato Celery Essence

4 cups chicken stock
1/2 bunch celery, washed,
    trimmed, and diced
1 cup canned tomatoes, drained
    and chopped

1 slice onion, diced
1/4 teaspoon thyme
1/2 teaspoon salt
salt and pepper to taste
4 sprigs parsley

Combine chicken stock and celery in saucepan. Bring mixture to boil. Lower heat. Cover and simmer for 30 minutes.

Combine tomatoes, onion, thyme, and salt in blender or food processor. Blend until smooth.

Strain celery broth. Discard celery. In saucepan, combine celery broth with tomato purée. Heat soup to boiling point. Add salt and pepper to taste.

Serve soup in warm tureen or warm individual soup bowls. Garnish with sprigs of parsley.

Makes four servings.

Chilled Carrot and Lettuce Bisque

4 cups chicken stock
5 medium carrots, shredded
2 tablespoons margarine
1 head Boston lettuce, shred-
    ded
1/4 cup scallions, minced

3 tablespoons margarine
1 cup sour cream
3/4 teaspoon chervil
4 egg yolks, beaten
salt and pepper to taste
sour cream

Heat chicken stock in saucepan to simmer. Remove from heat.

Combine carrots and 2 tablespoons margarine in saucepan. Sauté carrots for about 2 minutes. Transfer carrots to chicken stock.

Combine lettuce, scallions, and 3 tablespoons margarine in saucepan. Sauté for about 1 minute. Transfer vegetables to chicken stock. Stir in sour cream and chervil. Stir in beaten egg yolks.

Chill in covered container for about 4 hours. Add salt and pepper to taste.

Serve soup in glass bowls. Garnish with dollops of sour cream.

Makes six servings.

Chilled Squash and Carrot Bisque

3 medium yellow summer
    squash, sliced
2 medium carrots, chopped
1/2 green pepper, seeded and
    chopped
1 small onion, sliced
1 cup chicken stock

1/2 teaspoon salt
1 cup chicken stock
13 1/2 ounce can evaporated
    milk
salt and pepper to taste
parsley sprigs

Combine squash, carrots, green pepper, onion, 1 cup chicken stock, and salt in blender or food processor. Blend until smooth. Transfer mixture to mixing bowl. Stir in 1 cup chicken stock. Stir in evaporated milk.

Chill in covered container for about 4 hours. Add salt and pepper to taste.

Serve in glass bowls. Garnish with sprigs of parsley.

Makes six servings.

Gazpacho

4 tomatoes, quartered
1 cucumber, peeled and sliced
1 onion, sliced
1 green pepper, seeded and cut
    into chunks
1 clove garlic, crushed (op-
    tional)
2 tablespoons salad oil
2 tablespoons lemon juice
1/2 teaspoon salt

2–3 dashes cayenne
1/2 green pepper, chopped fine
1/2 cucumber, peeled and
    chopped fine
1/2 small onion, chopped fine
1 cup tomato juice
2 cups beef stock
salt to taste
cheese croutons

Combine tomatoes, sliced cucumber, sliced onion, green pepper chunks, garlic, salad oil, lemon juice, salt, and cayenne in blender or food processor. Blend until smooth.

Transfer to mixing bowl. Stir in chopped green pepper, chopped cucumber, chopped onion, tomato juice, and beef stock.

Chill in covered container for about 4 hours. Add salt to taste.

Serve in glass bowls. Garnish with cheese croutons.

Makes six servings.

Apricot Chicken Soup

4 ounces dried apricots,
  chopped
1 1/2 cups dry white wine
3 cups chicken stock
1/2 cup cooked chicken, diced

1 tablespoon chopped fresh
  basil
1/2 cup cooked rice, warm
salt and pepper to taste

Soak apricots in wine for 6 hours.

Combine chicken stock, chicken, and basil in saucepan. Add apricot and wine mixture. Bring to boil. Reduce heat and simmer for 25 minutes. Stir in rice. Add salt and pepper to taste.

Serve at once in warm tureen or warm individual soup bowls.

Makes four servings.

Frosty Mint Soup

1/4 cup fine barley
3 cups chicken stock
1 slice onion, minced
1/3 cup finely chopped fresh
  mint

1 1/2 cups yogurt
1/4 teaspoon salt
salt and pepper to taste
8 sprigs mint

Combine barley, chicken stock, and onion in saucepan. Bring mixture to boil. Lower heat and simmer for about 30 minutes, or until barley is tender. Remove saucepan from heat. Stir in mint. Allow to cool at room temperature. Add yogurt and salt. Stir until soup is smooth.

Chill in covered container for about 6 hours. Add salt and pepper to taste.

Serve soup in glass bowls or chilled mugs. Garnish with sprigs of mint.

Makes four servings.

Egg Drop Soup

6 cups chicken stock
10 ounce package chopped
   spinach
1/4 cup scallions, sliced very
   thin

3 eggs, beaten
3 cloves garlic, minced
1/4 teaspoon salt
salt and freshly ground white
   pepper to taste

Combine chicken stock, spinach, and scallions in saucepan. Bring mixture to boil. Lower heat. Cover and simmer for 5 minutes.

Combine eggs, garlic, and salt. Pour egg mixture into stock mixture in fine stream. Simmer soup for 2 minutes. Add salt and pepper to taste.

Serve at once in warm tureen or warm individual soup bowls.

Makes six servings.

Ginger Okra Soup

1 cup cut okra, fresh or frozen
1 cup water
1/4 teaspoon salt
4 cups chicken stock

1 tablespoon peeled, shredded
   ginger root
salt and pepper to taste

Combine okra, water, and salt in saucepan. Bring to boil. Lower heat. Cover and simmer for about 5 minutes, or until okra is tender.

Drain okra in colander. Refresh under cold running water. Set aside.

Combine chicken stock and ginger root in saucepan. Bring to boil. Lower heat to simmer. Add okra. Add salt and pepper to taste.

Serve soup at once in warm individual soup bowls.

Makes four servings.

Annie's Tips

Reserve drained cooking water to use in other recipes as vegetable water.

Chilled Zucchini Soup

4 medium zucchini, sliced
1 medium onion, chopped
1/2 green pepper, chopped
1 cup chicken stock
1/2 teaspoon salt

2 cups yogurt or sour cream
salt and pepper to taste
1 tomato, peeled, seeded, and
   chopped
snipped chives

Combine zucchini, onion, green pepper, chicken stock, and salt in blender or food processor. Blend until smooth.

Transfer to mixing bowl. Whisk in yogurt. Chill in covered container for about 4 hours. Add salt and pepper to taste.

Serve in glass bowls. Garnish with chopped tomato and snipped chives.

Makes six servings.

Minestrone

3 tablespoons salad oil
1 onion, chopped
1 clove garlic, minced
8 cups beef stock
2 medium carrots, diced
2 stalks celery and tops, sliced
1 cup string beans, snapped
1 cup tomatoes, chopped
1 cup chopped cabbage

1/4 cup minced parsley
1/8 teaspoon crushed red pepper (optional)
1/2 teaspoon thyme
1/2 teaspoon salt
4 ounces thin spaghetti, broken
1 pound can kidney beans
salt and pepper to taste
Parmesan cheese

Combine salad oil, onion, and garlic in large saucepan. Sauté for about 5 minutes.

Add beef stock, carrots, celery, string beans, tomatoes, cabbage, parsley, crushed red pepper, thyme, and salt. Bring to boil. Lower heat. Cover and simmer for about 15 minutes.

Bring soup to boil. Add spaghetti. Stir and cook for about 10 minutes. Stir in kidney beans. Add salt and pepper to taste.

Serve soup in warm tureen or warm individual soup bowls. Garnish with Parmesan cheese.

Makes eight servings.

Chilled Beet Borscht

2 tablespoons salad oil
1 onion, minced
2 pounds canned beets,
    drained, reserve juice
2 cups beef stock
1/4 teaspoon salt
1 tablespoon lemon juice

2 tablespoons honey
2 hard-boiled eggs, minced
1 cup sour cream
lemon juice or honey to taste
salt and pepper to taste
sour cream

Combine salad oil and onion in large saucepan. Sauté onion for about 3 minutes. Stir in reserved beet juice, beef stock, salt, lemon juice, and honey. Bring to boil. Lower heat. Cover and simmer for about 5 minutes.

Chop drained beets. Add beets to saucepan. Add either lemon juice or honey to taste.

Cool soup at room temperature. Whisk in minced egg and sour cream. Chill soup in covered container for about 4 hours. Add salt and pepper to taste.

Serve soup in glass bowls. Garnish with dollops of sour cream.

Makes eight servings.

Annie's Tips

Store chilled soups in glass jars in the refrigerator. Shake and serve.

Beef and Vegetable Soup

5 cups beef stock
2 carrots, diced
1 onion, chopped
2 stalks celery, diced
1 potato, peeled and diced
1 tomato, peeled, seeded, and
  chopped
1/2 cup peas

1/2 cup corn
1/4 teaspoon thyme
1/2 teaspoon salt
1/2 cup mushrooms, sliced
beef reserved from stock, cubed
2 tablespoons cornstarch
1/4 cup cold water
salt and pepper to taste

Combine beef stock with carrots, onion, celery, potato, tomato, peas, corn, thyme and salt in saucepan. Bring mixture to boil. Lower heat. Cover and simmer for about 20 minutes, or until vegetables are crisp tender. Add mushrooms and beef. Simmer for about 10 minutes.

Combine cornstarch and water. Stir cornstarch mixture into soup. Continue stirring. Simmer for about 10 minutes, or until soup has thickened. Add salt and pepper to taste.

Makes four servings.

Annie's Tips

Use a small glass jar with a tight lid to combine cornstarch and water; shake well.

Spinach Soup

4 cups chicken stock
1 medium red-skinned potato,
   peeled and diced
1 small onion, chopped
10 ounce package frozen
   chopped spinach

1/4 teaspoon thyme
1/2 teaspoon salt
salt and pepper to taste
Parmesan cheese, grated

Combine chicken stock, potato, onion, spinach, thyme, and salt in saucepan. Bring to boil. Lower heat. Cover and simmer for about 10 minutes, or until vegetables are tender. Add salt and pepper to taste.

Serve soup in warm tureen or warm individual soup bowls. Garnish with grated Parmesan cheese.

Makes six servings.

Tomato Bouillon Cup

2 1/2 cups bouillon
2 1/2 cups tomato juice
3 lemon slices
2 whole cloves

1 teaspoon chopped fresh basil
1/2 teaspoon sugar
salt and pepper to taste
bread sticks

Combine bouillon, tomato juice, lemon slices, cloves, basil, and sugar in saucepan. Bring to boil. Lower heat. Cover and simmer for about 5 minutes. Add salt and pepper to taste.

Strain soup through fine sieve.

Serve soup in bouillon cups with bread sticks.

Makes six servings.

Pear and Leek Soup

4 tablespoons margarine or
 salad oil
2 cups chopped leek
1 pound can pears, packed in
 juice

4 cups chicken stock
1/2 teaspoon summer savory
1/4 teaspoon salt
salt and white pepper to taste
croutons

Combine margarine and leek in saucepan. Sauté leek for about 3 minutes, or until tender.

Transfer leek to blender or food processor. Add pears, with juice. Blend until smooth.

Transfer to saucepan. Add chicken stock, summer savory, and salt. Bring to boil. Lower heat. Cover and simmer for about 20 minutes. Add salt and white pepper to taste.

Serve soup in warm tureen or warm individual soup bowls. Garnish with croutons.

Makes six servings.

Chilled Lemon Soup

1 cup chicken stock
4 tablespoons lemon juice
1/2 cup cooked rice
1/4 teaspoon salt
1/2 cup yogurt

3 cups chicken stock
1 hard-boiled egg, chopped fine
salt and pepper to taste
one strip of lemon peel (avoid
  white pith)

Combine 1 cup chicken stock, lemon juice, rice, and salt in blender or food processor. Blend until smooth. Transfer to mixing bowl. Whisk in yogurt, 3 cups chicken stock, and egg.

Chill soup in covered container for about 4 hours. Add salt and pepper to taste.

Serve in glass bowls. Garnish with strips of lemon peel.

Makes four servings.

Dried Mushroom Soup

1 ounce dried mushrooms,
  rinsed
1 cup warm water
1 onion, sliced
1 stalk celery, sliced
1 carrot, sliced thin

1/4 teaspoon salt
2 tablespoons flour
5 1/2 cups beef stock
1 tablespoon pearl barley
1/2 cup cooked white beans
salt and pepper to taste

Combine mushrooms and warm water in large covered saucepan. Set aside for 20 minutes. Put saucepan over heat. Bring to boil. Lower heat. Cover and simmer for about 20 minutes.

Drain mushrooms, reserving liquid. Chop and return to saucepan.

In blender or food processor combine reserved mushroom liquid with onion, celery, carrot, salt, and flour. Blend until smooth.

Transfer purée to saucepan. Add beef stock and barley. Bring mixture to boil. Lower heat. Cover and simmer for about 25 minutes. Stir in cooked white beans. Add salt and pepper to taste.

Serve soup in warm tureen or warm individual soup bowls.

Makes six servings.

Lamb and Vegetable Soup

4 cups lamb stock
2 carrots, diced
2 stalks celery, diced
1 medium onion, chopped
1 potato, peeled and diced
lamb reserved from stock,
   chopped

1/2 teaspoon salt
3 egg yolks, beaten
1/4 cup lemon juice
1/2 teaspoon paprika
salt to taste

In saucepan combine lamb stock, carrots, celery, onion, and potato. Bring mixture to boil. Lower heat. Cover and simmer for about 10 minutes, or until vegetables are crisp tender. Add reserved lamb and salt.

In mixing bowl combine 1 cup hot broth from saucepan, very slowly, with egg yolks. Add lemon juice and paprika to egg yolk mixture. Stir mixture into saucepan. Do not let soup boil. Add salt to taste.

Serve soup in warm tureen with loaf of crusty warm bread for hearty meal.

Makes four servings.

Chilled Pea Soup

10 ounce package frozen peas,
 broken into chunks
1/2 head lettuce, torn
1 slice onion
1/2 cup cold water

1/2 teaspoon salt
2 cups cold chicken stock
1/2 cup sour cream
salt and pepper to taste
2 tablespoons snipped chives

Combine frozen peas, lettuce, onion, water, and salt in blender or food processor. Blend until smooth. Transfer mixture to mixing bowl.

Stir in chicken stock and sour cream. Add salt and pepper to taste.

Serve at once in glass bowls. Garnish with snipped chives.
Makes four servings.

Chilled Lettuce and Watercress Soup

3 tablespoons salad oil
1 small onion
1 bunch watercress (about 2
 cups), reserve 4 sprigs for
 garnish
1 head Boston lettuce, torn
1/2 cup chicken stock

2 tablespoons ground almonds
1/2 teaspoon ground nutmeg
1/4 teaspoon salt
2 cups chicken stock
1 cup buttermilk or sour milk
salt and pepper to taste
toasted sliced almonds

Combine salad oil and onion in saucepan. Sauté onion for about 2 minutes. Add watercress and lettuce. Stir and cook for about 2 minutes.

Transfer to blender or food processor. Add 1/2 cup chicken stock. Blend until smooth.

Return purée to saucepan. Stir in ground almonds, nutmeg, salt and 2 cups chicken stock. Bring to boil. Lower heat. Cover and simmer for about 5 minutes. Stir in buttermilk.

Chill soup in covered container for about 5 hours. Add salt and pepper to taste.

Serve soup in glass or white bowls. Garnish with watercress sprigs and toasted sliced almonds.

Makes four servings.

Chilled Avocado Soup

1 cup chicken stock
2 medium avocados, seeded,
    peeled, and cut into chunks
2 tablespoons dry sherry
1/2 teaspoon salt
1 slice onion, chopped

1/4 teaspoon dillweed
1 cup yogurt
1 cup chicken stock
salt and pepper to taste
1 small avocado, peeled,
    seeded, and sliced

Combine 1 cup chicken stock, avocado chunks, dry sherry, salt, onion, and dillweed in blender or food processor. Blend until smooth. Transfer to mixing bowl. Stir in yogurt and 1 cup chicken stock.

Chill soup in covered container for about 4 hours. Add salt and pepper to taste.

Serve soup in glass bowls. Garnish with avocado slices.

Makes four servings.

Annie's Tips

Rest the glass bowl of soup on a bed of crushed ice, preferably inside a slightly larger glass bowl.

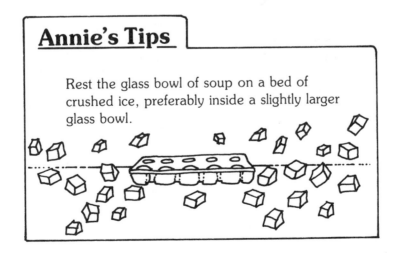

Vichyssoise

3 tablespoons salad oil
2 onions, chopped
2 cups chicken stock
4 medium potatoes, peeled and
   sliced

1/2 teaspoon salt
2 cups evaporated milk
1 cup yogurt
salt and pepper to taste
snipped chives

Combine salad oil and onion in saucepan. Sauté onion for about 3 minutes. Add chicken stock, potatoes, and salt. Bring to boil. Lower heat. Cover and simmer for about 15 minutes, or until potatoes are tender.

Transfer potato mixture to blender or food processor, in batches if necessary. Blend until smooth.

Transfer potato purée to mixing bowl. Whisk in evaporated milk and yogurt.

Chill soup in covered container for about 4 hours. Add salt and pepper to taste.

Serve soup in chilled bowls. Garnish with snipped chives.

Makes six servings.

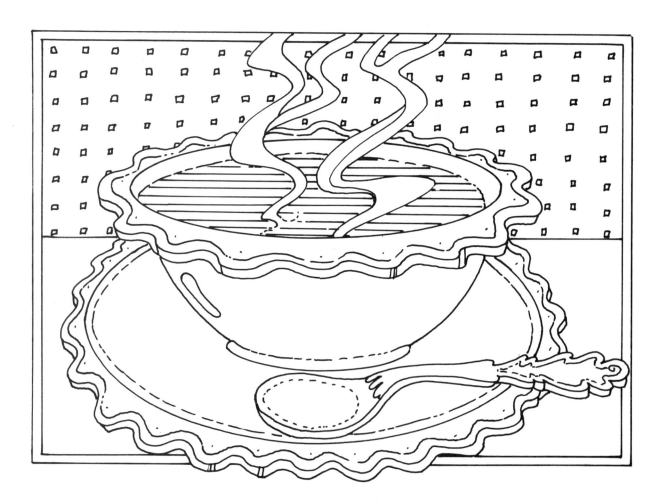

Basil Soup

4 tablespoons margarine
3/4 cup thinly sliced scallions,
  including green tops
4 cups chicken stock
2 tomatoes, peeled, seeded, and
  chopped

1/2 cup rice
1/2 teaspoon salt
3 cups chopped fresh basil
salt and pepper to taste

Combine margarine and scallions in saucepan. Sauté scallions for about 3 minutes, or until tender. Add chicken stock, tomatoes, and rice. Bring to boil. Lower heat. Cover and simmer for about 20 minutes, or until rice is tender. Add salt and basil. Simmer for about 10 minutes. Add salt and pepper to taste.

Serve soup in warm tureen or warm individual soup bowls.

Makes four servings.

Winter Squash Soup

2 cups water
1 small onion, diced
3 carrots, sliced
1 acorn squash, peeled, seeded,
  and cut into cubes
1/2 teaspoon salt

2 cups beef stock
1 tablespoon lime juice
2 tablespoons honey
1 cup cooked fine noodles
salt and pepper to taste
grated Parmesan cheese

Combine water, onion, carrots, squash, and salt in saucepan. Bring to boil. Lower heat. Cover and simmer for about 15 minutes.

Transfer vegetable mixture to blender or food processor, in batches if necessary. Blend until smooth.

Return the purée to saucepan. Stir in beef stock, lime juice, and honey. Bring to boil. Lower heat. Cover and simmer for about 10 minutes. Stir in noodles. Add salt and pepper to taste.

Serve soup in warm tureen or warm individual soup bowls. Garnish with grated Parmesan cheese.

Makes four servings.

Scotch Broth

1 1/2 quarts lamb stock
1 pound lamb trimmings, fat
  removed
5 tablespoons barley, rinsed
2 carrots, diced
2 onions, diced

2 stalks celery. diced
1 leek, sliced
1 teaspoon salt
salt and pepper to taste
4 tablespoons chopped parsley

Combine lamb stock and lamb trimmings in kettle. Bring mixture to boil. Skim off froth as it rises. Add barley, carrots, onions, celery, leek, and salt. Lower heat. Cover kettle and simmer for about 1 hour and 30 minutes. Add salt and pepper to taste.

Serve soup in warm tureen with loaf of crusty, warm bread for hearty meal. Garnish with chopped parsley.

Makes six to eight servings.

Annie's Tips

Draw a spoon across the surface of the hot liquid to skim froth.

Consommé with Avocado

3 cups clam juice
3 cups consommé

1/3 cup dry sherry
1 small avocado, sliced

Combine clam juice, consommé, and dry sherry in saucepan. Simmer for 2 minutes.

Put 2 or 3 slices of avocado in each warm soup bowl. Pour soup over avocado slices.

Makes six servings.

Chilled Broccoli Chowder

10 ounce package frozen
   chopped broccoli, cooked (do
   not drain)
1 slice onion, chopped
1 cup chicken stock
1/2 teaspoon salt

2 cups chicken stock
1 cup light cream
2 medium potatoes, peeled,
   diced, and boiled
salt and pepper to taste
grated cheese

Combine broccoli, onion, 1 cup chicken stock, and salt in blender or food processor. Blend until smooth.

Pour mixture into mixing bowl. Stir in 2 cups chicken stock, light cream, and potatoes.

Chill soup in covered container for about 4 hours. Add salt and pepper to taste.

Serve soup in glass bowl. Garnish with grated cheese.

Makes four servings.

Annie's Tips

Cold soup requires more seasoning than hot soup. Taste test the soup after chilling.

Cream Sherry Consommé

2 cups consommé
1/4 cup dry sherry

2 tablespoons currants or
   raisins
1 1/2 cups light cream

Combine consommé, sherry, and currants in saucepan. Bring to boil. Lower heat and simmer for 5 minutes. Stir in light cream.

Serve at once in warm soup bowls or mugs.

Makes four servings.

Eggplant Soup Parmigiana

3 tablespoons salad oil
1 medium onion, chopped
1 clove garlic, minced (optional)
1 medium eggplant, peeled and chopped
2 cups chicken stock
1 cup tomato juice

1/2 teaspoon salt
1/4 cup minced parsley
1/2 teaspoon dried thyme, crushed
salt and pepper to taste
4–6 ounces Mozzarella cheese, shredded

Combine salad oil, onion, and garlic in saucepan. Sauté for about 2 minutes. Add eggplant, chicken stock, tomato juice, salt, parsley, and thyme. Bring to boil. Lower heat. Cover and simmer for about 30 minutes. Add salt and pepper to taste.

Ladle soup into four ovenproof bowls. Top each bowl with portion of cheese. Bake soup in preheated 400 degree oven for about 10 minutes, or until cheese is melted.

Makes four servings.

Cream Fruit Consommé

3 tablespoons margarine
1 small onion, diced
1 apple, cored, peeled, and diced
1/4 cup apple juice
dash paprika

1/4 teaspoon salt
3 cups consommé
1 cup heavy cream
salt and pepper to taste
sliced fresh apples or pears

Combine margarine and onion in saucepan. Sauté onion for about 2 minutes. Add diced apple and sauté for about 3 minutes.

Transfer mixture to blender or food processor. Add apple juice, paprika, and salt. Blend until smooth.

Return purée to saucepan. Add consommé. Heat to boil. Lower heat. Stir in cream. Add salt and pepper to taste. Heat to simmer. Do not boil.

Serve consommé in bouillon cups with side dish of sliced fresh fruit.

Makes six servings.

Onion Soup

4 tablespoons salad oil
2 pounds onions, sliced thin
2 tablespoons flour
6 cups consommé
1/2 teaspoon paprika
1/2 teaspoon salt

salt and pepper to taste
6 slices French bread, toasted
  with garlic butter
6-8 ounces imported Swiss
  cheese, shredded

Combine salad oil and onions in large saucepan. Sauté onions for about 10 minutes. Stir in flour. Add consommé, paprika, and salt. Bring to boil. Lower heat. Cover and simmer for about 20 minutes. Add salt and pepper to taste.

Transfer soup to six ovenproof bowls. Place one slice of toasted bread on top of each bowl of soup. Top toast with some of shredded cheese.

Place bowls in preheated 400 degree oven for about 10 minutes, or until cheese is melted and golden.

Serve soup at once.

Makes six to eight servings.

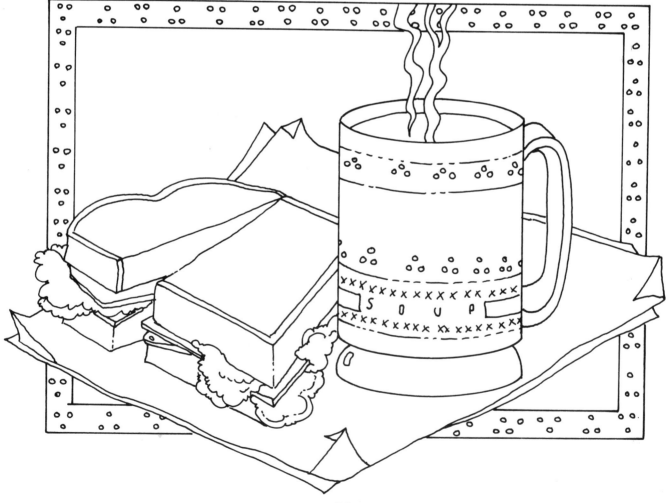

VEGETARIAN SOUPS

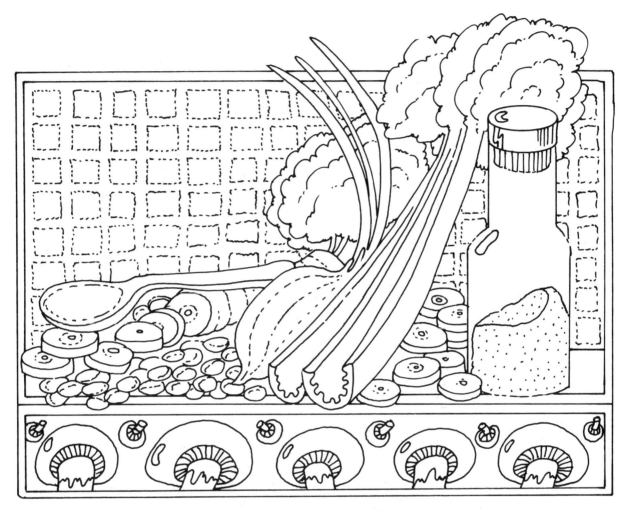

Vegetable Barley Soup

4 1/2 cups vegetable stock
1/2 cup medium barley
1/4 teaspoon crushed dried
  thyme

2 carrots, diced
1 potato, peeled and diced
1 small onion, chopped
salt and pepper to taste

In saucepan combine vegetable stock, barley, and thyme. Bring to boil. Lower heat. Cover and simmer for about 60 minutes. Stir occasionally. Add carrots, potato, and onion.

Cover and simmer for about 20 minutes, or until vegetables and barley are tender. Add salt and pepper to taste.

Serve soup in warm tureen or warm individual soup bowls.

Makes four servings.

Broccoli and Mushroom Soup

3 tablespoons margarine
1 small onion, minced
10 ounce package frozen
  chopped broccoli
1 cup fresh minced mushrooms
1 cup vegetable stock
1/4 teaspoon salt

1/2 teaspoon tarragon, crushed
2 cups light cream or half-and-
  half
1/2 cup dry white wine
salt and pepper to taste
4 fresh mushrooms, sliced thin

Combine margarine and onion in saucepan. Sauté onion for about 3 minutes. Add broccoli, mushrooms, vegetable stock, salt, and tarragon. Bring to boil. Lower heat. Cover and simmer for about 10 minutes. Stir in light cream and wine. Heat to simmer. Do not boil. Add salt and pepper to taste.

Serve soup in warm tureen or warm individual soup bowls. Garnish with sliced mushrooms.

Makes four servings.

Brussels Sprout and Cheese Soup

3 tablespoons margarine
1 onion, chopped
2 cups Brussels sprouts,
  trimmed
1 cup vegetable water

1/4 teaspoon salt
2 cups milk
1 cup grated cheddar cheese
salt and pepper to taste
croutons

Combine margarine and onion in saucepan. Sauté onion for about 2 minutes. Stir in Brussels sprouts. Continue to sauté for about 3 minutes.

Transfer to blender or food processor. Add vegetable water and salt. Blend until smooth.

Return purée to saucepan. Stir in milk and cheese. Heat to simmer. Stir and simmer for about 5 minutes. Do not boil. Add salt and pepper to taste.

Serve soup in warm tureen or warm individual soup bowls. Garnish with croutons.

Makes four servings.

Vegetable Soup with Eggs

1 large onion, chopped
3 tablespoons margarine or
   salad oil
2 cups cauliflower, sliced thin
2 tomatoes, peeled, seeded, and
   chopped
3 carrots, sliced thin
1/3 cup tomato paste

1 large potato, peeled and diced
1 cup peas
2 cups vegetable water
2 cups tomato juice
1 teaspoon salt
salt and pepper to taste
4 eggs

In saucepan sauté onion in margarine for about 2 minutes. Add cauliflower, tomatoes, carrots, and tomato paste. Simmer mixture for about 3 minutes. Add potato, peas, vegetable water, tomato juice, and salt. Bring to boil. Lower heat and simmer for about 20 minutes, or until vegetables are just tender. Add salt and pepper to taste.

Carefully add eggs to soup. Cover saucepan and poach eggs until they are set.

Serve at once in warm individual soup bowls with one egg and some vegetables in each bowl.

Makes four servings.

Annie's Tips

To make vegetable water, reserve the water from steamed vegetables in a covered jar in the refrigerator.

Cheddar Cheese Soup

1 cup vegetable stock
1 small onion, sliced
2 carrots, sliced
2 tablespoons parsley flakes
3 tablespoons flour
1/4 teaspoon salt
1 cup vegetable stock

2 cups milk
2 cups shredded sharp cheddar
   cheese
dash of cayenne
salt and white pepper to taste
3 tablespoons imitation bacon
   bits

Combine 1 cup vegetable stock, onion, carrots, parsley, flour, and salt in blender or food processor. Blend until smooth.

Transfer to saucepan. Heat mixture. Stir in 1 cup vegetable stock, milk, cheddar cheese, and cayenne. Continue stirring until cheese is melted, about 5 minutes. Add salt and pepper to taste.

Serve soup in warm tureen or warm individual soup bowls. Garnish with imitation bacon bits.

Makes four servings.

Chilled Orange Carrot Soup

1 pound carrots, sliced
3 inch strip orange peel (avoid
   pith)
1 small onion, sliced
1/2 teaspoon salt
2 cups water

1/4 teaspoon ground ginger
1/4 teaspoon ground cinnamon
1 cup orange juice
1 cup lemon yogurt
salt and pepper to taste
1 carrot, shredded

Combine sliced carrots, orange peel, onion, salt, and water in saucepan. Bring to boil. Lower heat. Cover and simmer for about 15 minutes, or until carrots are tender.

Transfer to blender or food processor, in batches if necessary. Blend until smooth.

Transfer purée to mixing bowl. Stir in ginger, cinnamon, orange juice, and yogurt.

Chill soup in covered container for about 4 hours. Add salt and pepper to taste.

Serve soup in glass bowls. Garnish with shredded carrot.

Makes four servings.

Chilled Cucumber Soup

1 medium cucumber
2 tablespoons fresh parsley,
  chopped
1/4 cup celery leaves, chopped
1 slice onion, chopped
1 tablespoon snipped dill
1 cup sour milk

1 cup sour cream
1 cup sour milk
1 tablespoon lemon juice
salt to taste
additional sour cream for garnish

Cut 4 thin slices from cucumber. Peel the remainder, seed, and cut into chunks.

Combine cucumber chunks in blender or food processor with celery leaves, onion, dill, and 1 cup sour milk. Blend until smooth.

Transfer mixture to mixing bowl. Whisk in sour cream, 1 cup sour milk, lemon juice, and salt.

Chill soup in covered container for about 3 hours.

Serve soup in glass bowls. Garnish with cucumber slices and dollops of sour cream.

Makes four servings.

Annie's Tips

To prepare sour milk, combine one table-spoon of white vinegar with whole milk to equal 1 cup. Let it stand for 5 minutes.

Iced Pea Soup

10 ounce package frozen peas
1 medium potato, peeled, cut
   into chunks, and boiled crisp
   tender
1 slice onion, chopped
1 cup vegetable stock

1 cup lemon yogurt
1 cup vegetable stock
salt and pepper to taste
2 tablespoons chopped fresh
   mint (1 tablespoon dried)

Do not defrost peas. Break frozen peas into chunks. Combine peas, potato, onion, and 1 cup vegetable stock in blender or food processor. Blend until smooth.

Transfer to mixing bowl. Whisk in 1 cup vegetable stock and yogurt. Add salt and pepper to taste.

Serve at once in glass bowls. Garnish with chopped mint.

Makes four servings.

Annie's Tips

Sprinkle dried herbs with water 10 minutes before using.

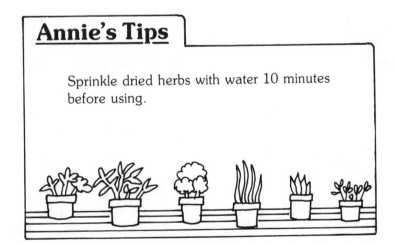

Creamy Pea Soup

1 medium potato, peeled,
   sliced, and boiled crisp
   tender
2 cups fresh peas, or 10 ounce
   package frozen peas
3/4 cup vegetable water
2 tablespoons salad oil
1 tablespoon fresh snipped
   parsley

1/2 teaspoon dried thyme
1 slice onion
1 cup vegetable water
salt and pepper to taste
1 cup sour cream
1/4 pound fresh mushrooms,
   sliced thin

Combine potato, fresh or frozen peas, 3/4 cup vegetable water, salad oil, parsley, thyme, and onion in blender or food processor. Blend until smooth. Transfer mixure to saucepan. Stir in 1 cup vegetable water. Simmer mixture for 5 minutes. Add salt and pepper to taste. Whisk in sour cream.

Serve soup in warm tureen. Garnish with sliced mushrooms.

Makes four servings.

Mushroom Barley Soup

1 cup water
1 small onion, sliced
1 medium potato, peeled and
   sliced thin
1/3 cup fine barley
2 tablespoons dried mushroom
   flakes, rinsed

5 cups vegetable stock
1/4 teaspoon salt
1/8 teaspoon pepper
1/4 cup pastina
salt and pepper to taste
sour cream
snipped chives

Combine water, onion, and potato in blender or food processor. Blend until smooth.

Transfer purée to saucepan. Add barley, dried mushrooms, vegetable stock, salt, and pepper. Bring to boil. Lower heat. Cover and simmer for about 1 hour and 15 minutes, or until barley is tender. Stir in pastina. Cover and simmer for about 20 minutes. Add salt and pepper to taste.

Serve soup in warm tureen or warm individual soup bowls. Garnish with dollop of sour cream and snipped chives.

Makes four servings.

Chilled Tomato Vegetable Soup

1 pound tomatoes, canned or
    fresh
4 medium carrots, sliced
2 stalks celery, chopped
1/2 medium green pepper,
    chopped
1 tablespoon chopped fresh
    basil

1 small onion, chopped
1/2 tablespoon chopped fresh
    thyme
2 cups vegetable stock
1 cup orange juice
1/4 teaspoon salt
salt and pepper to taste
slivers of orange peel

Combine tomatoes, carrots, celery, green pepper, onion, basil, and thyme in blender or food processor. Blend until smooth.

Transfer to mixing bowl. Stir in vegetable stock, orange juice, and salt.

Chill soup in covered container for about 4 hours. Add salt and pepper to taste.

Serve soup in glass bowls. Garnish with orange peel.

Makes four to six servings.

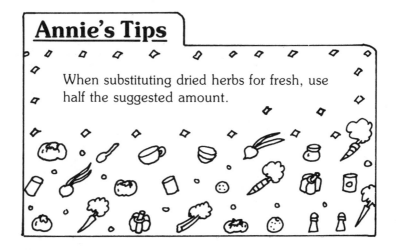

Annie's Tips

When substituting dried herbs for fresh, use half the suggested amount.

Dilled Potato and Onion Soup

4 large potatoes, peeled and
  diced
1 onion, chopped
2 cloves garlic, minced (optional)
1/2 teaspoon salt

3 cups vegetable water
1 cup milk
1/2 cup snipped dill
salt and pepper to taste
3 tablespoons imitation bacon
  bits

Combine potatoes, onion, garlic, salt, and vegetable water in saucepan. Bring mixture to boil. Lower heat. Cover and simmer for about 15 minutes. With slotted spoon remove half cooked potatoes from saucepan. Combine potatoes with milk in blender or food processor. Blend until smooth. Add potato purée and dill to saucepan. Simmer for about 5 minutes. Add salt and pepper to taste.

Serve soup in warm tureen or warm individual soup bowls. Garnish with imitation bacon bits.

Makes four servings.

64

Corn Chowder

1 large potato, peeled and
   sliced
1 cup water
1 small onion, sliced
1/2 teaspoon salt
2 tablespoons melted margarine
   or salad oil

2 tablespoons flour
3 cups cooked corn, fresh or
   canned
1 cup vegetable water
2 cups milk
salt and pepper to taste
cheese croutons

Combine potato, water, onion, and salt in covered saucepan. Bring mixture to boil. Lower heat. Cover and simmer until vegetables are crisp tender, about 10 minutes.

Transfer potato mixture to blender or food processor. Add melted margarine and flour. Blend until smooth.

Return potato purée to saucepan. Bring mixture to boil. Lower heat and stir in corn, vegetable water, and milk. Add salt and pepper to taste. Heat to simmer.

Serve soup at once in warm tureen or warm individual soup bowls. Garnish with cheese croutons.

Makes four servings.

Cold Beet and Cucumber Soup

3 cups buttermilk or sour milk
1 cup sour cream
1 pound can beets, chopped (do
   not drain)
1 cup cucumber, peeled,
   seeded, and chopped
1 tablespoon snipped dill

2 tablespoons minced scallions
1/2 teaspoon salt
3 tablespoons lemon juice
3 tablespoons sugar
3 hard-boiled eggs, chopped
salt and pepper to taste
sour cream garnish

In mixing bowl whisk together milk and sour cream. Stir in beets, cucumbers, dill, scallions, and salt. In small bowl combine lemon juice and sugar. Stir lemon juice mixture into milk mixture. Add eggs.

Chill soup in covered container for about 5 hours. Add salt and pepper to taste.

Serve soup in glass bowls. Garnish with dollops of sour cream.

Makes six servings.

Cool Cucumber and Red Onion Soup

1 tablespoon snipped dill
1/4 teaspoon salt
1/8 teaspoon white pepper
2 medium cucumbers, peeled
   and sliced thin
2 red onions, sliced thin
2 tablespoons snipped dill

additional salt
2 cups sour cream
1 tablespoon honey
2 tablespoons lemon juice
salt and pepper to taste
snipped dill

Combine 1 tablespoon snipped dill, 1/4 teaspoon salt, and white pepper in crock or saucepan. Place one quarter of sliced cucumber on top, then one quarter of sliced onions. Do not mix. Sprinkle salt and about 1/2 tablespoon snipped dill over layered vegetables.

Repeat layers using all vegetables and dill. Lightly sprinkle salt over each layer.

Combine sour cream and honey. Spread sour cream mixture on top layer.

Cover and chill for about 8 hours. Stir in lemon juice. Add salt and pepper to taste.

Serve soup in glass bowls. Garnish with snipped dill.

Makes four servings.

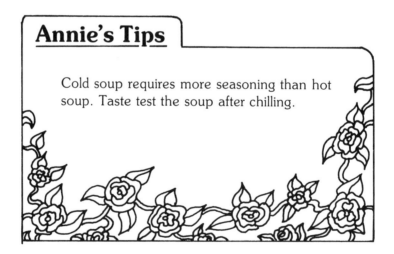

Annie's Tips

Cold soup requires more seasoning than hot soup. Taste test the soup after chilling.

Red Bean Soup With Rice

5 cups vegetable water
1/2 cup long grain rice
1/4 teaspoon salt
4 cups water

1/2 pound red kidney beans
1/4 teaspoon salt
salt and pepper to taste
honey

Combine 5 cups vegetable water, rice, and salt in saucepan. Bring to boil. Lower heat. Cover and simmer for about 1 hour and 30 minutes.

At same time, combine 4 cups water, red kidney beans, and salt in separate saucepan. Bring to boil. Lower heat. Cover and simmer for about 1 hour and 30 minutes.

Combine rice and beans in one large saucepan. Stir and blend. Simmer mixture, stirring occasionally, for about 40 minutes. Soup will be very thick. Add salt and pepper to taste.

Serve in warm individual soup bowls, with honey drizzled on top.

Makes six servings.

Chilled Artichoke Soup With Endive

9 ounce package frozen
   artichoke hearts
1 cup water
1/2 teaspoon salt
2 tablespoons margarine
1/2 pound endive, trimmed and
   torn
1 small onion, sliced

1/2 teaspoon sugar
1 egg yolk
1 cup light cream or half-and-
   half
2 cups vegetable stock
salt and pepper to taste
torn endive

Combine artichokes, water, salt, and margarine in saucepan. Bring to boil. Lower heat. Cover and simmr for about 8 minutes.

Transfer to blender or food processor. Add endive, onion, and sugar. Blend until smooth. Add egg yolk and blend.

Transfer purée to mixing bowl. Stir in light cream and vegetable stock.

Chill soup in covered container for about 4 hours. Add salt and pepper to taste.

Serve soup in chilled bowls. Garnish with torn endive.

Makes six servings.

Iced Green Bean Soup

10 ounce package frozen green
  beans
1 cup tomato juice
2 tablespoons fresh chopped
  basil
1 slice onion

1/2 teaspoon salt
1 egg yolk
1 cup tomato juice
2 cups sour milk
salt and pepper to taste
parsley sprigs

Combine green beans, 1 cup tomato juice, basil, onion, and salt in a blender or food processor. Blend until smooth. Add egg yolk.

Transfer to mixing bowl. Stir in 1 cup tomato juice and sour milk. Add salt and pepper to taste.

Serve soup at once in glass bowls. Garnish with sprigs of parsley.

Makes four servings.

Chilled Golden Squash Soup

2 yellow summer squash, sliced
3 tomatoes, cut into eighths,
  and cored
1 small onion, sliced
1 small green pepper, seeded
  and diced
1/4 teaspoon dried thyme

1/4 teaspoon dried basil
1 teaspoon salt
2 cups vegetable stock
1 cup orange juice
salt and freshly ground pepper
  to taste
snipped parsley

Combine squash, tomatoes, onion, green pepper, thyme, basil, and salt in blender or food processor. Blend until smooth.

Transfer to mixing bowl. Stir in vegetable stock and orange juice.

Chill in covered container for about 4 hours. Add salt and pepper to taste.

Serve in glass bowls. Garnish with parsley.

Makes six servings.

Chilled Cauliflower Soup

10 ounces frozen cauliflower
1 cup vegetable water
1 medium potato, peeled and
  sliced thin
1 slice onion, diced

1/4 teaspoon salt
2 cups buttermilk or sour milk
salt and pepper to taste
chopped fresh chives

Remove cauliflower from the freezer. Separate frozen florets.

Combine vegetable water, potato, and onion in saucepan. Bring to boil. Lower heat. Cover and simmer for about 5 minutes, or until just tender.

Transfer vegetable mixture to blender or food processor. Add cauliflower and salt. Blend until smooth.

Transfer purée to mixing bowl. Whisk in buttermilk. Chill in covered container for about 4 hours. Add salt and pepper to taste.

Serve soup in glass bowls. Garnish with chopped fresh chives.

Makes four servings.

Cream of Mushroom Soup

1 pound mushrooms, soaked,
  wiped, and trimmed
3 cups vegetable stock, heated
  in saucepan
1 cup vegetable stock
2 scallions, sliced

1 medium potato, peeled,
  sliced, and boiled crisp
  tender
1/2 teaspoon salt
freshly ground pepper to taste
3 egg yolks
1 cup evaporated milk

Reserve 6 mushrooms for garnish.

Combine 1 cup vegetable stock, mushrooms, scallions, potato, salt, and pepper in blender or food processor. Blend until smooth. Add mixture to hot stock in saucepan. Simmer for 5 minutes. Whisk egg yolks in mixing bowl. Whisk evaporated milk into egg yolks. Whisk continuously while adding 1 cup hot mixture from saucepan. Stir this mixture into saucepan. Cook over medium heat, stirring continuously, until soup is very hot. Do not boil.

Slice reserved mushrooms. Add mushrooms to soup. Add salt and pepper to taste.

Serve soup in warm tureen or warm individual soup bowls.

Makes six servings.

Chilled Green Summer Soup

1 cucumber, sliced
1 avocado, peeled, seeded, and
  cut into chunks
4 scallions, sliced
1/4 teaspoon salt

3 tablespoons lime juice
1 1/2 cups vegetable water
1 1/2 cups yogurt
salt and pepper to taste
celery leaves

Combine cucumber, avocado, scallions, salt, and lime juice in blender or food processor. Blend until smooth.

Transfer to mixing bowl. Whisk in vegetable water and yogurt.

Chill soup in covered container for about 4 hours. Add salt and pepper to taste.

Serve soup in glass bowls. Garnish with celery leaves.

Makes four servings.

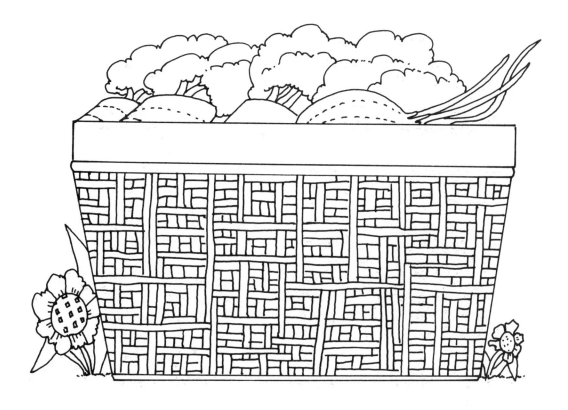

Rice Soup

2 tablespoons salad oil
1 small onion, diced
6 ounce package seasoned long
    grain and wild rice
3 cups vegetable water

3 cups vegetable stock
1 cup tomatoes, crushed
2 tablespoons dried mushroom
    flakes, rinsed
salt and pepper to taste

Combine salad oil and onion in large saucepan. Sauté onion for about 2 minutes. Add seasoned rice, vegetable water, vegetable stock, tomatoes, and dried mushrooms. Bring to boil. Lower heat. Cover and simmer for about 30 minutes. Add salt and pepper to taste.

Serve soup in warm tureen or warm individual soup bowls. Makes six servings.

Sweet Potato Soup

1 onion, chopped
3 tablespoons margarine or
    salad oil
3 tomatoes, peeled, seeded, and
    chopped
2 tablespoons chopped fresh
    parsley
1 pound sweet potatoes, peeled
    and sliced

1 cup sour milk
1 quart vegetable stock or
    vegetable water
1/4 cup cold water
2 tablespoons cornstarch
salt and pepper to taste
1/4 cup shredded coconut

In saucepan sauté onion in margarine for about 2 minutes. Add tomatoes and parsley. Simmer mixture over low heat for about 5 minutes. Add sweet potatoes. Cover and simmer for about 5 minutes. In blender or food processor combine vegetable mixture with sour milk. Blend until smooth. Reserve purée. Pour vegetable stock into saucepan. Heat to boil. Combine water and cornstarch. Lower heat to simmer. Stir in cornstarch mixture. Continue stirring until stock has thickened slightly. Stir in purée. Cover and simmer for about 5 minutes. Do not boil. Add salt and pepper to taste.

Serve soup in warm tureen or warm individual soup bowls. Garnish with shredded coconut.

Makes four servings.

Chilled Celery Soup

4 cups vegetable water
4 stalks celery, with tops, sliced
1 onion, sliced
1/4 teaspoon thyme
4 sprigs parsley
1 bay leaf
1/4 cup rice

1/2 teaspoon celery salt
3 eggs, beaten
2 tablespoons lemon juice
salt and white pepper to taste
1 lemon, sliced thin
celery leaves

Combine vegetable water, celery, onion, thyme, parsley, bay leaf, rice, and celery salt in large saucepan. Bring to boil. Lower heat. Cover and simmer for about 25 minutes.

Remove bay leaf. Strain through fine sieve over mixing bowl. Transfer cooked vegetable mixture to blender or food processor. Add 1 cup of reserved liquid. Blend until smooth. Transfer purée to mixing bowl containing reserved liquid.

Combine eggs and lemon juice in separate mixing bowl. Beat until light and fluffy. Whisk egg mixture into vegetable mixture.

Chill soup in covered container for about 4 hours. Add salt and pepper to taste.

Serve soup in glass or white bowls. Garnish with lemon slices and top with celery leaves.

Makes six servings.

Creamed Spinach Soup

2 tablespoons salad oil
1 small onion, chopped
2 cups vegetable stock
9-10 ounce package frozen
    creamed spinach, removed
    from pouch

1 cup light cream or half-and-
    half
salt and pepper to taste

Combine salad oil and onion in saucepan. Sauté onion for about 2 minutes.

Add vegetable stock and spinach. Stir and bring to simmer. Lower heat. Cover and simmer for about 10 minutes. Stir in light cream. Heat to simmer. Do not boil. Add salt and pepper to taste.

Serve in warm tureen or warm individual soup bowls.

Makes four servings.

Celery Cabbage Soup

2 cups vegetable water or
 Green Vegetable Stock
2 tablespoons salad oil
1 onion, diced
2 tablespoons salad oil
1 stalk celery, with top, sliced

1 bunch celery cabbage, sliced
1/4 cup cooked rice
1/2 teaspoon celery salt
2 cups yogurt or sour cream
salt and white pepper to taste
minced parsley

Combine 2 tablespoons salad oil and onion in saucepan. Sauté onion for about 2 minutes. Add 2 tablespoons salad oil, celery, and celery cabbage. Stir and sauté mixture for about 5 minutes.

Transfer to blender or food processor. Add rice and celery salt. Blend until smooth.

Return purée to saucepan. Stir in yogurt and vegetable water. Heat soup to simmer. Do not boil. Add salt and pepper to taste.

Serve soup in warm tureen or warm individual white soup bowls. Garnish with minced parsley.

Makes six servings.

Chilled Avocado and Watercress Soup

2 avocados, seeded, peeled,
  and cut into chunks
1 bunch watercress, about 2
  cups, reserve 4 sprigs for garnish
1 cup vegetable water
1 tablespoon chopped scallions

2 parsley sprigs
1/4 teaspoon salt
2 cups yogurt
2 tablespoons lemon juice
dash cayenne
salt to taste
chopped watercress leaves

Combine avocados, watercress, vegetable water, scallions, parsley and salt in blender or food processor. Blend until smooth.

Transfer purée to mixing bowl. Whisk in yogurt, lemon juice, and cayenne. Chill soup in covered container for about 2 hours. Add salt to taste.

Serve soup in glass or white bowls. Garnish with chopped watercress leaves.

Makes four servings.

Vegetable Chowder

2 tablespoons salad oil
1 onion, diced
4 cups vegetable water
2 carrots, sliced
2 stalks celery, diced
2 medium zucchini, cubed
1 cup green beans, snapped
2 tomatoes, peeled, seeded, and
  chopped

2 potatoes, peeled and diced
1/2 teaspoon salt
1/2 teaspoon thyme
1/2 teaspoon marjoram
2 tablespoons quick-cooking
  farina
1/2 cup light cream
salt and pepper to taste
minced parsley

Combine salad oil and onion in saucepan. Sauté onion for about 3 minutes. Add vegetable water, carrots, celery, zucchini, green beans, tomatoes, potatoes, salt, thyme, marjoram, and farina. Bring to boil. Lower heat. Cover and simmer for about 15 minutes, or until vegetables are tender. Stir in light cream. Add salt and pepper to taste.

Serve soup in warm tureen or warm individual soup bowls. Garnish with minced parsley.

Makes six servings.

Pumpkin Soup

2 tablespoons salad oil
1 small onion, minced
1 stalk celery, minced
1 pound can or 2 cups cooked
  pumpkin, cubed
2 cups vegetable stock
2 tablespoons honey

1/2 teaspoon salt
1/4 teaspoon nutmeg
1 cup light cream or evaporated
  milk
salt and pepper to taste
minced parsley

Combine salad oil, onion, and celery in saucepan. Sauté for about 3 minutes. Add pumpkin, vegetable stock, honey, salt, and nutmeg. Bring to boil. Lower heat. Cover and simmer for about 10 minutes. Slowly stir in light cream. Add salt and pepper to taste. Heat to simmer. Do not boil.

Serve soup in warm tureen or warm individual soup bowls. Garnish with minced parsley.

Makes four servings.

Tomato Rice Soup

2 tablespoons salad oil
1 onion, chopped
1 cup vegetable water
2 carrots, sliced
1/4 teaspoon salt
1/4 teaspoon basil
1/4 teaspoon parsley flakes
2 1/2 cups vegetable stock

1/4 cup rice
1 pound tomatoes, peeled,
  seeded, and chopped (about
  1 1/2 cups)
2 tablespoons tomato paste
1 tablespoon honey
salt and white pepper to taste
minced basil

Combine salad oil and onion in saucepan. Sauté onion for about 3 minutes. Add vegetable water and carrots. Bring to boil. Lower heat. Cover and simmer for about 10 minutes.

Transfer mixture to blender or food processor. Add salt, basil, and parsley. Blend until smooth.

Return purée to saucepan. Add vegetable stock, rice, tomatoes, tomato paste, and honey. Bring to boil. Lower heat. Cover and simmer for about 25 minutes, or until rice is tender. Add salt and pepper to taste.

Serve soup at once in warm tureen or warm individual soup bowls. Garnish with minced basil.

Makes four servings.

Chilled Blue Cheese Soup With Caviar

2 ounces blue cheese, crumbled
1 cup milk
1/4 teaspoon dried chives
1/4 teaspoon dried thyme
1/8 teaspoon white pepper

2 cups sour cream or yogurt
additional milk, if desired
salt and pepper to taste
4 ounce jar red caviar

Combine blue cheese, milk, chives, thyme, and pepper in blender or food processor. Blend until smooth.

Transfer to mixing bowl. Whisk in sour cream. Check consistency and add more milk if desired. Chill in covered container for about 6 hours. Add salt and pepper to taste.

Serve soup in glass or white bowls. Garnish each serving with dollop of caviar.

Makes four servings.

Annie's Tips

To substitute fresh herbs for dried, double the suggested amount.

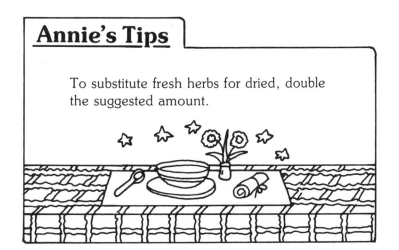

Alfalfa Sprout Soup With Mushrooms

4 cups vegetable stock
1 tablespoon soy sauce
1/4 pound mushrooms, soaked,
   wiped, and sliced very thin
1 cup alfalfa sprouts

1/4 cup cooked shrimp, minced
   (optional)
salt and pepper to taste
2 tablespoons minced parsley

Combine vegetable stock, soy sauce, and mushrooms in saucepan. Bring to boil. Lower heat. Cover and simmer for about 3 minutes. Add sprouts. Cover and simmer for about 2 minutes. Stir in cooked shrimp. Add salt and pepper to taste.

Serve soup at once in warm tureen or warm individual soup bowls. Garnish with minced parsley.

Makes four servings.

Corn Soup

3 cups vegetable stock
8-9 ounce can cream style corn
1/2 teaspoon salt
2 tablespoons cornstarch
3 tablespoons vegetable stock
   or water

2 egg whites, beaten until
   frothy
2 tablespoons milk
salt and pepper to taste
minced parsley or alfalfa
   sprouts

Heat vegetable stock in saucepan to boil. Lower heat to simmer.

Combine corn and salt in blender or food processor. Blend until smooth.

Combine cornstarch and vegetable stock. Set aside. Combine egg whites and milk. Set aside.

Add puréed corn to saucepan. Increase heat. Stir continuously until mixture comes to boil. Lower heat slightly. Stir in cornstarch mixture. Continue to stir until mixture thickens. Add salt and pepper to taste.

Remove saucepan from heat. Without stirring, pour egg white mixture into saucepan very slowly. Stir once.

Serve soup in warm tureen or warm individual soup bowls. Garnish with parsley or sprouts.

Makes four servings.

Strips of Cucumber Soup

1 tablespoon dried mushroom
   flakes, rinsed
4 cups warm vegetable stock

1 medium cucumber
1 tablespoon soy sauce
salt and pepper to taste

Combine dried mushrooms and vegetable stock in saucepan. Set aside for about 30 minutes.

Peel cucumber and cut into quarters lengthwise. Remove seeds. Slice vertically in julienne strips. Set aside.

Add soy sauce to mushroom and stock mixture. Heat to boil. Lower heat. Cover and simmer for about 2 minutes. Add cucumber. Cover and simmer for about 2 minutes. Add salt and pepper to taste.

Serve soup at once in warm tureen or warm individual soup bowls.

Makes four servings.

Schav

1 pound schav (sorrel, sour
   grass), washed
1/2 onion, grated
6 cups water
1 teaspoon salt
1 tablespoon lemon juice
2 tablespoons sugar

sugar or lemon juice to taste
2 eggs
1 cup sour cream
salt and pepper to taste
1 hard-boiled egg, minced
sour cream

Combine schav, onion, water, and salt in large saucepan. Bring to boil. Lower heat. Cover and simmer for about 1 hour.

Combine lemon juice and sugar. Add to saucepan. Continue to simmer for about 15 minutes. Add either sugar or lemon juice to taste. Remove saucepan from heat.

Beat eggs in mixing bowl. Stirring constantly, slowly add 1 cup hot soup. Stir in 1 cup sour cream. Stir mixture into saucepan.

Chill soup in covered container for about 5 hours. Add salt and pepper to taste.

Serve soup in glass bowls. Garnish with minced egg and sour cream.

Makes six servings.

Gazpacho

3 ripe tomatoes, peeled, seeded, and chopped
1 cucumber, sliced
1 green pepper, seeded and cut into chunks
1 medium onion, sliced
1 clove garlic, crushed (optional)
2 tablespoons lemon juice

2 tablespoons salad oil
1 cup tomato juice
2–3 dashes cayenne pepper
salt to taste
1 cucumber, finely chopped
1 green pepper, finely chopped
1 onion, finely chopped
salt to taste
1/4 cup chopped fresh parsley

Combine tomatoes, cucumber slices, green pepper chunks, onion slices, garlic, lemon juice, and salad oil in blender or food processor. Blend until smooth.

Transfer to mixing bowl. Stir in tomato juice, cayenne pepper, and salt to taste. Stir in chopped vegetables.

Chill in covered container for about 4 hours. Add salt to taste.

Serve in glass bowls. Garnish with chopped parsley.

Makes four servings.

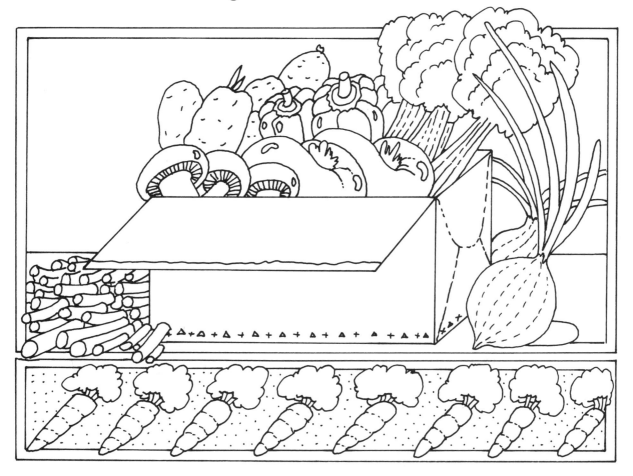

Split Pea Soup

5 cups vegetable water and/or
    vegetable stock
1 cup split peas
1 carrot, diced
1 onion, diced

1 stalk celery, diced
1/2 teaspoon salt
1/4 cup pastina
salt and pepper to taste
minced parsley

Combine vegetable water, split peas, carrot, onion, celery, and salt in large saucepan. Bring to boil. Lower heat. Cover and simmer for about 2 hours. Stir occasionally. Add pastina. Cover and simmer for about 15 minutes. Add salt and pepper to taste.

Serve soup in warm tureen or warm individual soup bowls. Garnish with minced parsley.

Makes four servings.

Hearty Vegetable Soup

4 cups vegetable stock
1 onion, chopped
3 tablespoons parsley, minced
2 carrots, diced
2 stalks celery and tops,
    chopped
2 potatoes, peeled and diced
2 zucchinis, diced

1/2 pound mushrooms, soaked,
    wiped, trimmed, and
    chopped
1 bay leaf (optional)
1/2 teaspoon salt
2 tablespoons cornstarch
1/4 cup water
salt and pepper to taste

In saucepan combine vegetable stock, onion, parsley, carrots, celery, potato, zucchini, mushrooms, bay leaf, and salt. Bring mixture to boil. Lower heat. Cover and simmer for about 20 minutes. Remove bay leaf. Combine cornstarch and water. Stir cornstarch mixture into saucepan. Continue stirring until soup has thickened slightly. Add salt and pepper to taste.

Serve soup in warm tureen or warm individual soup bowls.

Makes four servings.

SEAFOOD SOUPS

Red Cod Chowder

2 tablespoons salad oil
1 onion, minced
6 cups Puréed Fish Stock
2 cups water
3 medium potatoes, peeled and
  cubed

1/2 teaspoon salt
2 pounds codfish filets, cut into
  strips
1 tablespoon lemon juice
salt and pepper to taste

Combine salad oil and onions in large saucepan. Sauté onions for about 2 minutes, or until just tender. Add Puréed Fish Stock, water, potatoes, and salt. Bring to boil. Lower heat. Cover and simmer for about 10 minutes. Add fish and lemon juice. Cover and simmer for about 10 minutes, or until potatoes are tender. Add salt and pepper to taste.

Serve soup in warm tureen or warm individual soup bowls.

Makes four servings.

Shrimp Gumbo

2 cups Basic Fish Stock
3 tablespoons salad oil
1 onion, diced
1/2 green pepper, diced
2 cups sliced okra, fresh or
  frozen
2 stalks celery, sliced

2 1/2 cups water
1 teaspoon salt
3/4 pound small shrimp, peeled
  and deveined
1 cup cooked rice
salt and pepper to taste

Combine salad oil, onion, and green pepper in large saucepan. Sauté for about 3 minutes, or until just tender. Add okra, celery, water, and salt. Bring to boil. Lower heat. Cover and simmer for about 10 minutes. Stir in shrimp and Basic Fish Stock. Cover and simmer for about 5 minutes. Stir in cooked rice. Add salt and pepper to taste.

Serve soup at once in warm tureen or warm individual soup bowls.

Makes six servings.

Vegetable Clam Chowder

1 cup clam juice
1 cup water
8 ounce can tomato sauce
1 pound can tomatoes
2 medium potatoes, diced
1 green pepper, diced
2 carrots, diced
2 onions, diced
2 stalks celery, diced
1 tablespoon marjoram

1 teaspoon thyme
1/2 teaspoon salt
1/4 teaspoon pepper
1 teaspoon sugar
14–16 ounces canned minced
  clams
1 cup corn, fresh or frozen
salt and pepper to taste
chopped parsley

Combine clam juice, water, tomato sauce, tomatoes, potatoes, green pepper, carrots, onions, celery, marjoram, thyme, salt, pepper, and sugar in large saucepan. Bring to boil. Lower heat. Cover and simmer for about 20 minutes, or until vegetables are crisp tender. Add minced clams and corn. Simmer soup for about 10 minutes. Add salt and pepper to taste.

Serve soup in warm tureen or warm individual soup bowls. Garnish with chopped parsley.

Makes six servings.

Shrimp and Crab Soup

1 cup Basic Fish Stock
1/4 cup onion, minced
1 stalk celery, minced
3 tablespoons flour
1 teaspoon salt
4 tablespoons margarine

1 quart milk
6 ounces frozen crabmeat
6 ounces frozen or fresh tiny
   shrimp
salt and white pepper to taste
chopped parsley

Combine margarine, onion, and celery in large saucepan. Sauté for about 3 minutes. Stir in flour and salt. Stir in Basic Fish Stock and milk. Stir continuously until mixture thickens. Do not boil.

Add crabmeat and shrimp. Heat soup to simmer. Simmer for about 10 minutes. Do not boil. Add salt and white pepper to taste.

Serve soup in warm tureen or warm individual soup bowls. Garnish with chopped parsley.

Makes six servings.

Herbed Spinach Soup

3 cups Basic Fish Stock
2 tablespoons salad oil
1 onion, diced
1 tablespoon flour
1 cup clam juice
10 ounce package frozen
   chopped spinach

1/4 teaspoon salt
2 tablespoons parsley flakes
1/4 teaspoon tarragon
salt and pepper to taste
grated lemon rind

Combine salad oil and onion in saucepan. Sauté onion for about 2 minutes. Stir in flour. Add Basic Fish Stock and clam juice. Bring to boil. Add frozen spinach, salt, parsley flakes, and tarragon. Return to boil. Lower heat. Cover and simmer for about 15 minutes. Add salt and pepper to taste.

Serve soup in warm tureen or warm individual soup bowls. Garnish with grated lemon rind.

Makes four servings.

Chilled Shrimp Bisque

3/4 cup Basic Fish Stock or
   cooking water from shrimp
2 tablespoons salad oil
1 small onion, diced
1 stalk celery and top, diced
14–16 ounces shrimp, cooked,
   peeled, diveined, and sliced if
   large
1/4 teaspoon paprika

1/2 teaspoon salt
2 tablespoons flour
1 cup evaporated milk
3 cups milk
2–3 dashes cayenne
salt to taste
alfalfa sprouts or minced
   parsley

Combine salad oil, onion, and celery in saucepan. Sauté vegetables for about 3 minutes, or until just tender.

Transfer to blender or food processor. Add shrimp, Basic Fish Stock, paprika, salt, and flour. Blend. Add evaporated milk. Blend until smooth.

Transfer to mixing bowl. Stir in milk and cayenne.

Chill soup in covered container for about 4 hours. Add salt to taste.

Serve bisque in glass bowls. Garnish with alfalfa sprouts or minced parsley.

Makes six servings.

Crab Gumbo

2 cups Basic Fish Stock
4 tablespoons margarine or
  salad oil
1 small onion, sliced
1/4 cup minced green pepper
1/4 cup raw rice
3 medium tomatoes, peeled and
  diced

1 cup sliced okra
6–7 ounces crabmeat, flaked
1/2 teaspoon Worcestershire
  sauce
salt and pepper to taste
parsley sprigs

Combine margarine, onion, and green pepper in large saucepan. Sauté for about 5 minutes. Add Basic Fish Stock and rice. Bring to boil. Lower heat. Cover and simmer for about 20 minutes. Stir in tomatoes, okra, crabmeat, and Worcestershire sauce. Simmer soup for about 20 minutes. Add salt and pepper to taste.

Serve soup in warm tureen or warm individual soup bowls. Garnish with parsley sprigs.

Makes six servings.

Chilled Lobster Bisque

2 tablespoons salad oil
1 stalk celery, with top, diced
1/2 green pepper, diced
1 onion, diced
1 cup tomato juice
3 ounce package cream cheese
  and chives, softened
1/4 teaspoon salt

1 whole pimiento, cut into
  chunks
dash cayenne
4 ounces cooked lobster,
  minced
2 cups sour cream or yogurt
salt and cayenne to taste
snipped chives

Combine salad oil, celery, green pepper, and onion in saucepan. Sauté mixture for about 5 minutes.

Transfer to blender or food processor. Add tomato juice, cream cheese, salt, pimiento, and cayenne. Blend until smooth.

Transfer purée to mixing bowl. Whisk in lobster and sour cream.

Chill soup in covered container for about 3 hours. Add salt and cayenne to taste.

Serve soup in white or glass bowls. Garnish with snipped chives.

Makes four servings.

Clam Bisque

4 tablespoons margarine or
   salad oil
1 small onion, minced
1 stalk celery, minced
4 tablespoons flour
1/2 teaspoon salt
dash cayenne
1/8 teaspoon dry mustard

2 teaspoons lemon rind
2 cups milk
14–16 ounces canned or fresh
   minced clams
2 cups milk
salt and pepper to taste
chopped parsley

Combine margarine, onion, and celery in saucepan. Sauté for about 5 minutes or until vegetables are tender. Stir in flour, salt, cayenne, dry mustard, and lemon rind. Slowly stir in 2 cups milk. Continue stirring until mixture has thickened slightly.

Combine 2 cups milk with minced clams in separate saucepan. Heat to simmer. Do not boil. Stir milk and clam mixture into first saucepan. Add salt and pepper to taste.

Serve bisque in warm tureen or warm individual soup bowls. Garnish with chopped parsley.

Makes four servings.

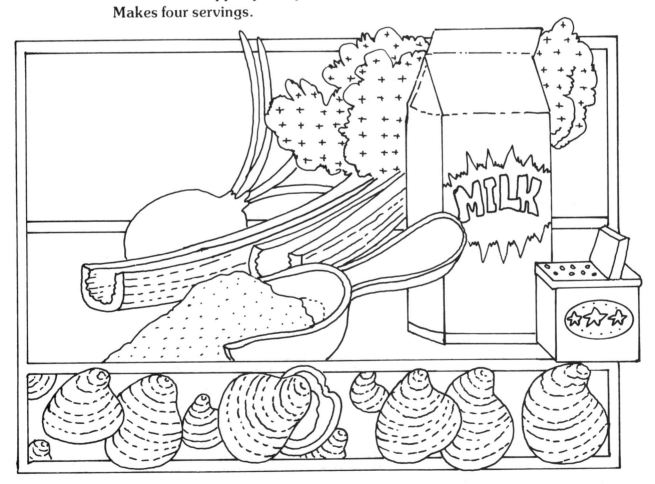

White Clam Chowder

2 tablespoons margarine or
  salad oil
1 onion, diced
2 medium potatoes, peeled and
  diced
1 cup clam juice

water
14–16 ounces canned or fresh
  minced clams
2 cups half-and-half or light
  cream
salt and pepper to taste

Combine margarine and onion in saucepan. Sauté onion for about 3 minutes. Add potatoes, clam juice, and enough water to cover potatoes. Bring to boil. Lower heat. Cover and simmer for about 15 minutes, or until potatoes are tender. Stir in clams and half-and-half. Heat soup to simmer. Do not boil. Add salt and pepper to taste.

Serve soup in warm tureen or warm individual soup bowls.

Makes four servings.

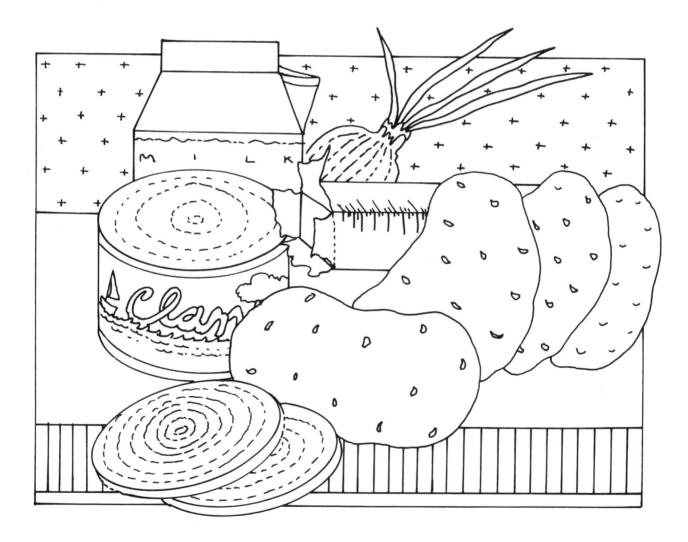

Red Clam Chowder

3 tablespoons salad oil or
  margarine
1 medium onion, chopped
2 carrots, chopped
1 stalk celery, chopped
1 green pepper, chopped
2 medium potatoes, peeled and
  diced

1 pound can tomatoes
1/4 teaspoon salt
2 cups water
1 cup clam juice
14–16 ounces canned or fresh
  minced clams
salt and pepper to taste

Combine salad oil, onion, carrots, celery, and green pepper in large saucepan. Sauté for about 3 minutes. Add potatoes, tomatoes, salt, water, and clam juice. Bring to boil. Lower heat. Cover and simmer for about 15 minutes. Add clams. Cover and simmer for about 5 minutes. Add salt and pepper to taste.

Serve soup in warm tureen or warm individual soup bowls.

Makes six servings.

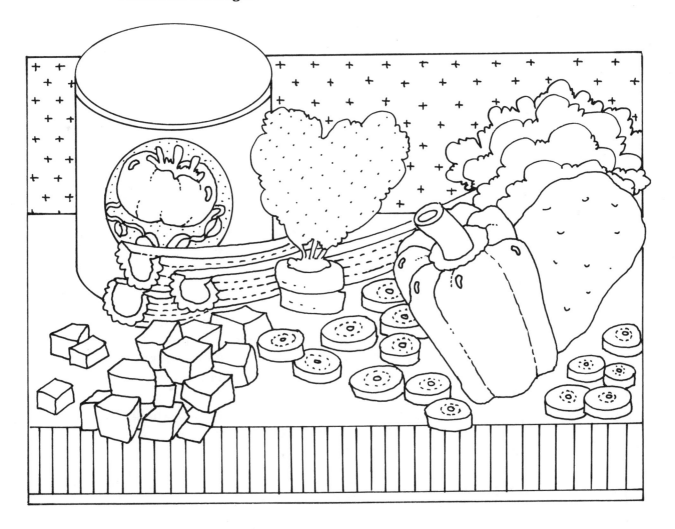

Chilled Clam and Avocado Soup

1 cup White Fish Stock
2 medium avocados, peeled,
    seeded, and cut into chunks
1 cup clam juice
1 cup evaporated milk or light
    cream

2 tablespoons dry sherry
14–16 ounces canned or fresh
    minced clams
salt and pepper to taste
chopped parsley

Combine avocados and clam juice in blender or food processor. Blend until smooth.

Transfer avocado mixture to mixing bowl. Stir in White Fish Stock, evaporated milk, dry sherry, and minced clams.

Chill soup in covered container for about 4 hours. Add salt and pepper to taste.

Serve soup in chilled bowls. Garnish with chopped parsley.

Make four servings.

Bouillabaisse

6 cups Basic Fish Stock
3 tablespoons salad oil
2 onions, chopped
1 clove garlic, minced
2 cups crushed tomatoes
1 stalk celery and top, diced
1 carrot, diced
bouquet garni of 1 bay leaf and
    1/4 teaspoon fennel seed
1/2 teaspoon thyme
1/8 teaspoon saffron
2 tablespoons minced parsley

1 teaspoon salt
1/8 teaspoon cayenne
1 teaspoon dulse
3 pounds mixed prepared raw
    shellfish (shrimps, mussels,
    lobster, scallops, clams,
    oysters)
1/2 teaspoon white horseradish
2 tablespoons lemon juice
salt and pepper to taste
garlic croutons

Combine salad oil, onions, and garlic in large saucepan. Sauté for about 2 minutes. Add tomatoes, celery, carrot, bouquet garni, thyme saffron, parsley, Basic Fish Stock, salt, cayenne, and dulse. Bring to boil. Lower heat. Cover and simmer for about 15 minutes.

Remove and discard bouquet garni. Add prepared shellfish, horseradish, and lemon juice. Cover and simmer for about 10 minutes. Add salt and pepper to taste.

Serve soup in warm tureen with garlic-flavored croutons.

Makes eight servings.

Chilled Salmon Bisque

4 tablespoons margarine or
  salad oil
1 small onion, diced
1/2 green pepper, diced
1 cup canned salmon
1 cup milk or half-and-half
1 teaspoon salt

1/4 teaspoon paprika
2 1/2 cups half-and-half or
  evaporated milk
2 tablespoons dry sherry
salt and pepper to taste
1/4 cup minced green pepper

Combine margarine, onion, and green pepper in saucepan. Sauté for about 3 minutes, or until green pepper is tender.

Transfer mixture to blender or food processor. Add salmon and milk. Blend until smooth.

Transfer purée to saucepan. Stir in salt, paprika, and half-and-half. Stir and heat to simmer.

Cool soup at room temperature. Chill in covered container for about 4 hours. Add dry sherry and salt and pepper to taste.

Serve bisque in chilled bowls. Garnish with minced green pepper.

Makes four servings.

Oyster Soup

3 cups White Fish Stock
3 tablespoons salad oil
1 stalk celery, with top, minced
1 small onion, minced
1 clove garlic, finely chopped
  (optional)

2 tablespoons flour
1/4 teaspoon celery salt
8 ounces oysters, canned or
  fresh, shucked
salt and pepper to taste
minced parsley

Combine salad oil, celery, onion, and garlic. Sauté for about 5 minutes. Stir in flour. Stir until blended. Stir in White Fish Stock and celery salt. Bring to boil. Lower heat. Cover and simmer for about 10 minutes. Add oysters. Simmer for about 3 minutes. Add salt and pepper to taste.

Serve soup in warm tureen or warm individual soup bowls. Garnish with minced parsley.

Makes four servings.

Clam and Mushroom Soup

4 tablespoons margarine or
  salad oil
1/2 pound mushrooms, soaked,
  wiped, and sliced thin
3 tablespoons flour
2 cups clam juice
7–7 1/2 ounces canned or fresh
  minced clams

1 cup evaporated milk or light
  cream
1/2 teaspoon salt
1/4 teaspoon ground white pepper
1/8 teaspoon tarragon
salt and pepper to taste
ground paprika

Combine margarine with mushrooms in saucepan. Sauté mushrooms for about 5 minutes. Stir in flour. Stir in clam juice and minced clams. Continue stirring mixture until slightly thickened. Stir in evaporated milk, salt, pepper, and tarragon. Heat to just under boil. Do not boil. Add salt and pepper to taste.

Serve soup in warm tureen or warm individual soup bowls. Garnish with sprinkle of paprika.

Makes four servings.

Mushroom Bisque

3 tablespoons margarine or
   salad oil
3/4 pound mushrooms, soaked,
   wiped, and sliced
1 tablespoon flour
2 cups heated clam juice

1/2 cup half-and-half or
   evaporated milk
1 tablespoon dry sherry
1/4 pound mushrooms, soaked,
   wiped, and sliced very thin
salt and pepper to taste
minced parsley

Combine margarine and 3/4 pound mushrooms in saucepan. Sauté mushrooms for about 2 minutes. Stir in flour until blended. Stir in clam juice. Bring to boil. Lower heat. Cover and simmer for about 5 minutes.

Transfer mixture, in batches if necessary, to blender or food processor. Blend until smooth.

Transfer purée to saucepan. Stir in half-and-half, dry sherry, and 1/4 pound mushrooms. Simmer bisque for about 5 minutes. Do not boil. Add salt and pepper to taste.

Serve bisque in warm tureen or warm individual soup bowls. Garnish with minced parsley.

Makes four servings.

Fishyssoise

2 cups White Fish Stock
2 tablespoons margarine or
   salad oil
1 large onion
3 potatoes, peeled and sliced

1 cup cooked white fish, flaked
2 cups milk or half-and-half
salt and white pepper to taste
snipped chives or dill

Combine margarine and onion in saucepan. Sauté onion for about 2 minutes. Add potatoes and White Fish Stock. Bring to boil. Lower heat. Cover and simmer for about 20 minutes, or until potatoes are very tender.

Transfer mixture to blender or food processor. Blend until smooth.

Transfer purée to large mixing bowl. Stir in fish and milk.

Chill soup in covered container for about 4 hours. Add salt and white pepper to taste.

Serve soup in chilled bowls. Garnish with snipped chives or dill.

Makes four servings.

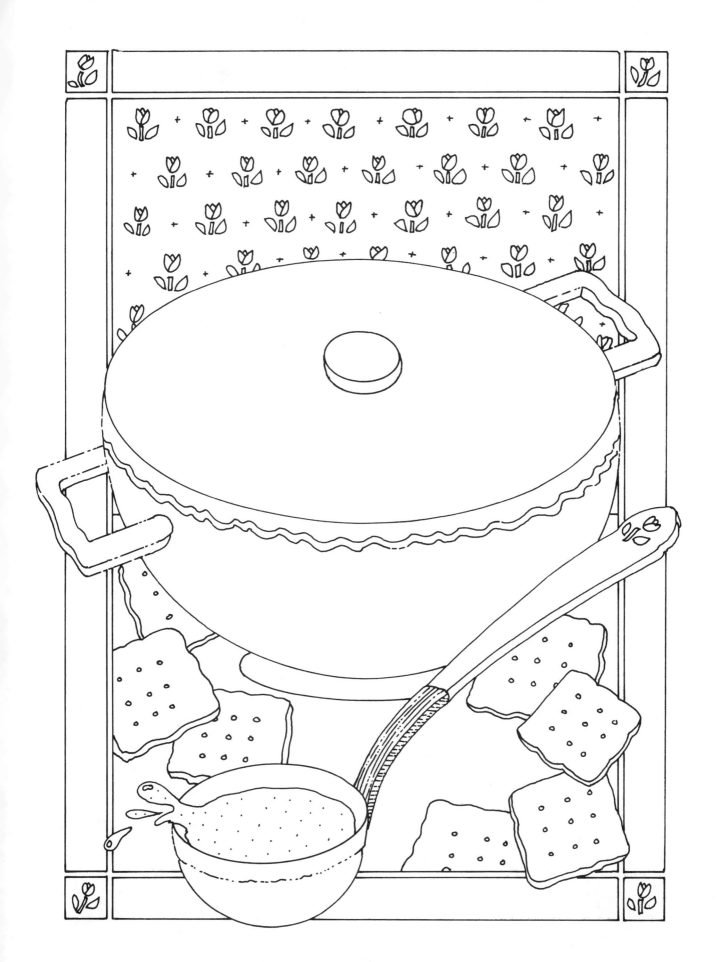

99

Oyster Spinach Potage

10 ounce package frozen
  creamed spinach
3 tablespoons margarine
2 tablespoons flour
1/2 teaspoon salt
1/2 teaspoon celery salt
1/8 teaspoon white pepper
1 tablespoon parsley flakes

2 cups milk
8 ounce can whole oysters, do
  not drain
1 cup light cream or half-and-
  half
1/2 cup dry white wine
salt and pepper to taste
thin lemon slices

Prepare frozen creamed spinach according to package directions. Set aside.

Combine margarine and flour in heavy saucepan. Stir until blended. Add salt, celery salt, and white pepper.

Add creamed spinach to saucepan. Stir in milk. Continue to stir over medium heat until blended. Add oysters and light cream. Heat to simmer. Do not boil. Stir in dry white wine. Add salt and pepper to taste.

Serve soup in warm tureen or warm individual soup bowls. Garnish with thin lemon slices.

Makes four servings.

Shrimp and Mushroom Chowder

2 tablespoons salad oil
1 onion, minced
1 cup clam juice
1 cup water
2 medium potatoes, peeled and
    diced
1/2 teaspoon salt

3/4 pound small shrimp, peeled
    and deveined
1 pound fresh mushrooms,
    soaked, wiped, and chopped
1 cup light cream or half-and-
    half
salt and pepper to taste
oyster crackers

Combine salad oil and onion in large saucepan. Sauté onion for about 3 minutes. Add clam juice, water, potatoes, and salt. Bring to boil. Lower heat. Cover and simmer for about 5 minutes.

Transfer about half of potatoes to blender or food processor. Add 1 cup of liquid from saucepan. Blend until smooth.

Return purée to saucepan. Add shrimp and mushrooms. Bring to boil. Lower heat. Cover and simmer for about 5 minutes, or until shrimp are pink. Stir in light cream. Heat to simmer. Do not boil. Add salt and pepper to taste.

Serve chowder in warm tureen or warm individual soup bowls with side dish of oyster crackers.

Makes four servings.

Creamed Mussels and Vegetable Chowder

3 cups White Fish Stock
2 tablespoons salad oil
1 medium onion, chopped
2 medium carrots, diced
2 stalks celery, diced
2 medium potatoes, diced

12 ounce can mussels and
    liquid or
2 quarts fresh mussels,
    prepared and cooked, with li-
    quid reserved
2 cups light cream
salt and pepper to taste

Combine salad oil and onion in large saucepan.
Sauté onions for about 3 minutes.
Add White Fish Stock, carrots, celery, and potatoes. Bring mixture to boil. Lower heat. Cover and simmer for about 15 minutes. Add mussels and liquid. Add light cream. Heat chowder to simmer. Do not boil.

Serve chowder in warm tureen or warm individual soup bowls.
Makes six servings.

Shellfish Gumbo

3 cups White Fish Stock
4 tablespoons salad oil
1 1/2 cups okra, fresh or
    defrosted frozen, sliced
1 onion, chopped
1/2 green pepper, chopped
1/4 teaspoon finely chopped
    garlic (optional)
1 tablespoon arrowroot or corn-
    starch
1 cup tomatoes, peeled and
    chopped
1 tablespoon minced parsley
1/2 teaspoon thyme

3/4 teaspoon salt
dash cayenne
1/2 pound raw tiny shrimp,
    fresh or frozen, peeled and
    deveined
6 ounces lump crabmeat
7–8 ounces minced clams,
    canned or fresh
8 ounces oysters, canned or
    fresh
salt and pepper to taste
1 cup hot cooked rice
minced parsley

Combine salad oil and okra in large saucepan. Sauté okra for about 3 minutes. Stir constantly. Add onion, green pepper, and garlic. Stir and sauté for about 5 minutes.

Combine arrowroot with about 1/4 cup of stock. Stir in White Fish Stock, arrowroot mixture, tomatoes, parsley, thyme, salt, and cayenne. Bring to boil. Add shrimp. Simmer for about three minutes. Add crabmeat, clams, and oysters. Simmer for about 3 minutes. Add salt and pepper to taste.

Serve soup in warm tureen with portion of rice in each warm individual soup bowl. Garnish with minced parsley.

Makes six servings.

FRUIT SOUPS

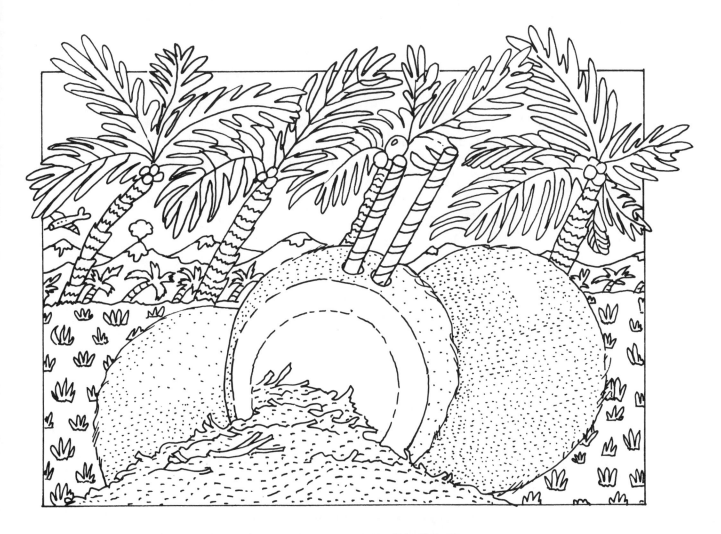

Chilled Yogurt Fruit Soup

1 pound can dark sweet cher-
ries in heavy syrup
3 tablespoons lemon juice

1 pound can sliced peaches,
drained
2 cups lemon yogurt
1 lemon, sliced very thin

Combine cherries with syrup and lemon juice in blender or food
processor. Blend until smooth. Add peaches. Blend until smooth.
Transfer fruit mixture to mixing bowl. Stir in yogurt.
Chill soup in covered container for about 4 hours.
Serve soup in glass bowls. Garnish with lemon slices.
Makes six servings.

Iced Orange Strawberry Soup

2 cups frozen strawberries, dry
  pack
1 cup water
1 cup orange juice

3 tablespoons Grand Marnier
  liqueur
1 cup strawberry yogurt
sprigs fresh mint
fresh strawberry slices

Cut frozen strawberries in half if they are large. Combine strawberries and water in blender or food processor. Blend until smooth. Transfer mixture to large mixing bowl. Whisk in orange juice, liqueur, and yogurt.

Serve soup at once in glass bowls. Garnish with sprigs of mint or fresh strawberry slices.

Makes four servings.

Annie's Tips

Instant homemade soups may be prepared in advance. Keep the soup chilled in an empty quart glass juice bottle. Shake well before serving.

Iced Strawberry Champagne Soup

2 cups frozen strawberries, dry
  pack
1 bottle chilled champagne

1 cup strawberry yogurt
lemon peel, finely grated

Cut strawberries in half if they are large. Put frozen strawberries in blender or food processor. Blend until smooth.

Divide strawberry slush between four glass bowls.

Let each diner help himself to champagne, stirring it into strawberry slush. Serve strawberry yogurt topped with lemon peel in side dish to be passed as garnish.

Makes four servings.

Creamy Tomato Soup

1 carrot, chopped
1 stalk celery, chopped
1 slice onion, chopped
2 tablespoons margarine or
    salad oil
1 tablespoon flour
2 cups tomatoes, fresh or
    canned, chopped

1 clove garlic, minced (op-
    tional)
1/2 teaspoon crushed thyme
1/4 teaspoon sugar
1/2 teaspoon salt
1 cup vegetable water
1 cup yogurt
salt and pepper to taste
parsley sprigs

In saucepan sauté carrot, celery, and onion in margarine for about 3 minutes. Add flour to vegetable mixture. Stir until well blended. Stir in tomatoes, garlic, thyme, sugar, and salt. Simmer for 5 minutes. Add vegetable water. Bring to boil. Lower heat and simmer for about 20 minutes.

Transfer to blender or food processor. Blend until smooth. Return to saucepan. Stir in yogurt. Add salt and pepper to taste. Heat to simmer. Do not boil.

Serve soup in warm tureen or warm individual soup bowls. Garnish with parsley sprigs.

Makes four servings.

CREAMY·TOMATO·SOUP

Rosé Broth with Mandarin Oranges

6 egg whites
1/4 teaspoon cream of tartar
1/2 teaspoon nutmeg
2 cups rosé wine
1 cup orange juice
2 cups water

11 ounce can mandarin orange
 segments, drained, reserve
 syrup
3 cinnamon sticks, cracked in
 half
3 tablespoons lemon juice
1 tablespoon cornstarch

In mixing bowl beat egg whites with cream of tartar and nutmeg. Beat until stiff. Cover mixing bowl and refrigerate.

Combine wine, orange juice, water, reserved syrup, and cinnamon sticks in saucepan. Bring mixture to boil. Lower heat. Simmer for about 4 minutes. Add orange segments to saucepan.

Combine lemon juice with cornstarch. Stir cornstarch mixture into saucepan. Stir constantly until broth thickens. Remove cracked cinnamon sticks and place in each serving bowl. Pour broth over cracked cinnamon sticks. Garnish with stiffly beaten egg whites.

Makes six servings.

Chilled Raspberry Soup

2 cups raspberries, fresh or
  frozen dry pack
1 tablespoon honey
1/2 cup dry red wine

1 cup raspberry yogurt
1 cup warm coconut milk
shredded coconut

Combine raspberries, honey, and wine in blender or food processor. Blend until smooth. Strain purée through fine sieve into mixing bowl. Stir in yogurt and coconut milk.

Chill soup in covered container for about 3 hours.

Serve soup in glass bowls. Garnish with shredded coconut.

Makes four servings.

Annie's Tips

Before using prepared chilled coconut milk, heat to blend.

Rhubarb and Strawberry Soup

4 cups fresh or frozen rhubarb,
   cut into 1 inch pieces
1 cup water
1/4 cup honey
2 cups fresh or frozen strawberries, hulled

1/2 teaspoon nutmeg
1/4 teaspoon salt
1 1/2 cups reserved fruit juice or
   orange juice
ladyfingers

Combine rhubarb and water in saucepan. Bring to boil. Lower heat. Cover and simmer for about 3 minutes.

Combine rhubarb mixture, honey, strawberries, nutmeg, and salt in blender or food processor. Blend until smooth.

Transfer to saucepan. Stir in fruit juice. Heat to simmer.

Serve soup in glass or white bowls with ladyfingers.

Makes six servings.

Cold Fresh Plum Soup

3 cups diced fresh plums
1 quart water
1/2 cup honey
2 tablespoons lemon juice
1/2 inch strip lemon peel

1 stick cinnamon
2 tablespoons cornstarch
1/4 cup cold water
salt and pepper to taste
sour cream

In saucepan combine plums, 1 quart water, honey, lemon juice, lemon peel, and cinnamon stick. Bring mixture to boil. Lower heat and simmer for about 20 minutes, or until plums are very soft. Remove lemon peel and cinnamon stick. Force mixture through food mill. Return mixture to saucepan.

Combine cornstarch and cold water. Stir cornstarch mixture into saucepan. Continue stirring. Bring mixture to boil. Lower heat. Simmer while stirring constantly until soup thickens slightly.

Cool soup at room temperature. Chill soup in covered container for about 6 hours. Add salt and pepper to taste.

Serve soup in glass bowls. Garnish with dollops of sour cream.

Makes six servings.

Chilled Sour Cherry Soup

3 cups water
1 cup granulated sugar
4 cups pitted sour cherries
1 tablespoon cornstarch

1/4 cup water
1/2 cup dry red wine
1/2 cup heavy cream
ground cinnamon

Combine water and sugar in saucepan. Bring mixture to boil. Boil for 3 minutes. Stir and wash down any sugar crystals clinging to sides of saucepan. Lower heat to simmer. Add sour cherries and simmer partially covered for about 35 minutes.

Combine cornstarch with 1/4 cup water. Stir cornstarch mixture into cherry mixture. Simmer for about 5 minutes.

Allow cherry mixture to cool at room temperature. Stir in wine and cream.

Chill soup in covered container for about 6 hours.

Serve soup in glass bowls. Garnish with ground cinnamon.

Makes four to six servings.

Annie's Tips

Use a brush dipped in cold water to wash down sugar crystals.

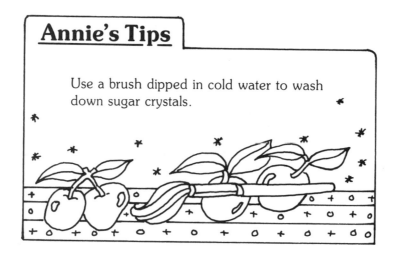

Chilled Honeydew Soup

1 large honeydew melon
6 ounce can frozen lime juice
    concentrate
2 tablespoons ground almonds
3 tablespoons lemon juice

1 teaspoon grated lemon rind
1 1/2 cups cold water
1 cup sour cream
thin slices of lime or fresh mint
    sprigs

Cut melon in half. Remove seeds and membrane. With melon-ball cutter, scoop out flesh from half of melon. Reserve melon balls in covered container in refrigerator.

Remove flesh from second half of melon.

Combine melon, lime juice concentrate, ground almonds, lemon juice, and lemon rind in blender or food processor. Blend until smooth.

Transfer to mixing bowl. Stir in cold water and sour cream. Chill soup in covered container for about 3 hours.

Before serving soup, stir in reserved melon balls. Serve soup in glass bowls. Garnish with lime slices or mint sprigs.

Makes four servings.

Annie's Tips

Rest the glass bowl of soup on a bed of crushed ice, preferably inside a slightly larger glass bowl.

Iced Peach Soup

4 cups peaches, or 20 ounce
   frozen dry pack, cut into
   chunks
1/2 cup water
3 tablespoons honey

1/4 teaspoon cinnamon
1/4 teaspoon curry powder
1/8 teaspoon cloves
1/4 teaspoon salt
2 1/2 cups cold dry white wine
thin slices of orange

Combine peaches, water, honey, cinnamon, curry powder, cloves, and salt in blender or food processor. Blend until smooth.

Transfer peach purée to mixing bowl. Whisk in wine.

Serve soup at once in glass soup bowls. Garnish each serving with slice of orange.

Makes six servings.

Annie's Tips

Instant homemade soups may be prepared in advance and kept chilled in the refrigerator. Shake well before serving.

Cold Cherry Wine Soup

1 can dark sweet cherries
   (16 1/2 ounces)
1 cup cherry wine
1 quart water
3 inches stick cinnamon

3 tablespoons small pearl
   tapioca
4 tablespoons honey
1 tablespoon lemon juice
2 egg yolks, beaten
1/2 lemon, sliced thin

Combine canned cherries and wine in blender or food processor. Blend until smooth.

In saucepan, combine cherry and wine mixture with water, stick cinnamon, tapioca, honey, and lemon juice. Bring mixture to boil. Lower heat and simmer for 10 minutes. Remove stick cinnamon.

In mixing bowl add 1 cup of hot liquid from saucepan, very slowly, to egg yolks. Stir egg yolk mixture into saucepan.

Remove saucepan from heat and allow to cool at room temperature. Chill soup in covered container for about 6 hours.

Serve soup in glass bowls. Garnish with lemon slices.

Makes six servings.

Iced Big Blue Soup

1 1/2 cups cold water
3 cups frozen blueberries, dry
   pack
1 teaspoon lemon juice

1 tablespoon honey
pinch of salt
heavy cream
fresh mint sprigs

Combine water, blueberries, lemon juice, honey, and salt in blender or food processor, in batches if necessary. Blend until smooth.

Pour soup at once into four glass bowls or glass mugs. Carefully pour cream down side of each bowl so thin layer floats on top of soup.

Garnish with fresh mint sprigs. Serve at once.

Makes four servings.

Chilled Plum Soup

1 pound 13 ounce can purple
   plums, drain, and reserve
   syrup
1 cup water
2/3 cup sugar
1 cinnamon stick
1/4 teaspoon white pepper
1/2 teaspoon lemon rind

salt and pepper to taste
1/2 cup dry red wine
1 tablespoon cornstarch
2 tablespoons brandy
1 cup sour cream
1/2 cup heavy cream
ground cinnamon
sour cream

Pit and chop drained plums. Combine plums and reserved syrup in saucepan. Add water, sugar, cinnamon stick, pepper, and lemon rind. Bring mixture to boil. Lower heat and simmer for 5 minutes. Remove cinnamon stick. Add salt and pepper to taste. Combine wine and cornstarch. Stir into saucepan. Continue stirring until mixture thickens. In small mixing bowl, whisk brandy and sour cream with 1 cup of hot soup. Stir mixture into saucepan. Stir in heavy cream. Allow soup to cool at room temperature. Chill soup in covered container for about 6 hours.

Serve soup in glass bowls. Garnish each bowl with dollop of sour cream and sprinkle of ground cinnamon.

Makes six servings.

Tropical Fruit Chowder

2 cups Coconut Milk
1 very ripe banana, mashed
1 cup half-and-half
1/2 cup crushed pineapple,
  drained
1 cup white grapes, cut into
  halves and seeded if
  necessary

2 tablespoons ground almonds
2 tablespoons Cointreau
1/4 teaspoon salt
1 banana, cut into chunks
salt to taste
shredded coconut

Combine mashed banana and Coconut Milk in saucepan. Heat to boil. Lower heat to simmer. Add half-and-half, pineapple, white grapes, ground almonds, Cointreau, and salt. Heat to simmer. Do not boil. Simmer for about 3 minutes. Add banana chunks. Add salt to taste.

Serve chowder in warm tureen or warm individual soup bowls. Garnish with shredded coconut.

Makes four servings.

Annie's Tips

Before using prepared chilled coconut milk, heat to blend.

Chilled Tomato Soup

1 cup tomato juice
1 tablespoon salad oil
3 tablespoons lemon juice
1 teaspoon Worcestershire
  sauce
1 slice onion
1 stalk celery, diced

1 tablespoon chopped fresh
  basil
1–2 dashes cayenne pepper
1/2 teaspoon salt
2 cups tomato juice
1 cup yogurt
salt and pepper to taste

Combine 1 cup tomato juice, salad oil, lemon juice, Worcestershire sauce, onion, celery, basil, cayenne pepper, and salt in blender or food processor. Blend until smooth. Transfer mixture to mixing bowl. Stir in 2 cups tomato juice and yogurt.

Chill soup in covered container for about 4 hours. Add salt and pepper to taste.

Serve soup in glass bowls. Garnish with additional chopped basil.

Makes four servings.

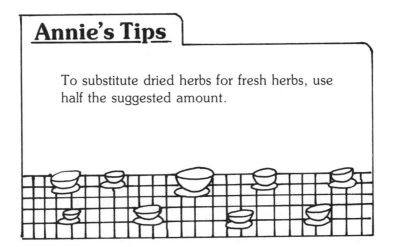

Annie's Tips

To substitute dried herbs for fresh herbs, use half the suggested amount.

Mixed Fruit Soup

12 whole dried apricots, diced
1 1/2 cups dry white wine
4 cups cold water
16 1/2 ounce can pitted cherries, chopped

16 ounce can peaches, chopped
8 ounce can pitted plums, diced
4 tablespoons lemon juice
1 lemon, sliced thin

Soak apricots in wine for 6 hours.

Combine apricot and wine mixture, with cold water in saucepan. Bring mixture to boil. Lower heat and simmer for about 30 minutes. Stir in cherries, peaches, plums, and lemon juice.

Simmer for 5 minutes.

Serve soup in warm tureen or warm individual soup bowls. Garnish with lemon slices.

Makes six servings.

Iced Mixed Melon Soup

4 cups mixed melon balls, or 20 ounce frozen dry pack
1/2 cup bread crumbs
1/4 cup ground almonds
1 tablespoon salad oil
2 tablespoons lemon juice
2 egg yolks

2 tablespoons chopped fresh mint
1 1/2 cups sour milk or buttermilk
salt and pepper to taste
4 sprigs fresh mint

Cut frozen melon balls into chunks. Reserve for later use.

Combine bread crumbs, almonds, salad oil, lemon juice, egg yolks, and chopped mint in blender or food processor. Blend until smooth. Add melon chunks. Blend until smooth.

Transfer mixture to mixing bowl. Whisk in milk. Add salt and pepper to taste.

Serve soup at once in glass bowls. Garnish each serving with sprig of mint.

Makes four servings.

Iced Anyberry Soup

2 cups frozen berries, dry pack   *2 tablespoons honey*
4 tablespoons lemon juice   *2 cups very cold water*
1/3 cup orange juice   *4 sprigs fresh mint*

Combine berries, lemon juice, orange juice, and honey in blender or food processor. Blend until smooth.

Transfer mixture to mixing bowl. Stir in very cold water.

Serve soup at once in glass bowls. Garnish each serving with sprig of mint.

Makes four servings.

Annie's Tips

To serve fruit soup as a dessert, add half the suggested amount of water.

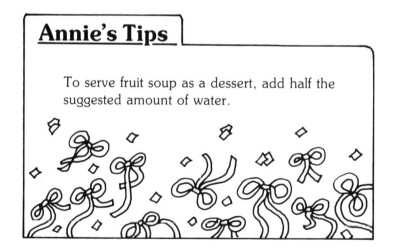

INDEXES

Hot Soups

Cold Soups

Time Index

Before starting any other preparations, assemble all of the needed ingredients.

Instant Homemade

Prepared in blender or food processor. Ready to serve at once.

Quick Soups

Prepared in 30 minutes or less.

Chilled Quick Soups

Prepared in 30 minutes or less. These soups require several hours chilling before serving. This also gives the flavors time to mingle.

Slow Cook Stocks and Soups

*Prepared using longer, slower, cooking
   time, perhaps as much as several
   hours.*

Weights and Measures

Customary

3 teaspoons = 1 tablespoon
4 tablespoons = 1/4 cup
5 1/3 tablespoons = 1/3 cup
12 tablespoons = 3/4 cup
16 tablespoons = 1 cup
2 cups = 1 pint
2 pints = 1 quart
4 quarts = 1 gallon
1 pound = 16 ounces
1 fluid ounce = 2 tablespoons
16 fluid ounces = 1 pint

Metric

1 liter = 1000 milliliters
1 liter = 10 deciliters
1 kilogram = 1000 grams

Equivalents

Customary

1/5 teaspoon = 1 milliliter
1 teaspoon = 5 milliliters
1 tablespoon = 15 milliliters
1/5 cup = 50 milliliters (approx.)
1 cup = 240 milliliters
1 pint = 470 milliliters
1 quart = .95 liter
1 gallon = 3.8 liters
1 fluid ounce = 30 milliliters
1 ounce dry weight = 28 grams
1 pound = 454 grams (approx. 1/2
   kilogram)

Metric

1 milliliter = .034 fluid ounce
1 liter = 1.06 quarts
1 liter = .264 gallon
1 gram = .035 ounce
1 kilogram = 2.205 pounds
   (35 ounces)